PENGUIN BOOKS — GREAT IDEAS

The Symposium

Plato

c. 429–347 BC

Plato

The Symposium

TRANSLATED BY
CHRISTOPHER GILL AND DESMOND LEE

PENGUIN BOOKS — GREAT IDEAS

PENGUIN BOOKS

Published by the Penguin Group
Penguin Books Ltd, 80 Strand, London WC2R 0RL, England
Penguin Group (USA) Inc., 375 Hudson Street, New York, New York 10014, USA
Penguin Group (Canada), 10 Alcorn Avenue, Toronto, Ontario, Canada M4V 3B2
(a division of Pearson Penguin Canada Inc.)
Penguin Ireland, 25 St Stephen's Green, Dublin 2, Ireland
(a division of Penguin Books Ltd)
Penguin Group (Australia), 250 Camberwell Road,
Camberwell, Victoria 3124, Australia (a division of Pearson Australia Group Pty Ltd)
Penguin Books India Pvt Ltd, 11 Community Centre,
Panchsheel Park, New Delhi – 110 017, India
Penguin Group (NZ), cnr Airborne and Rosedale Roads, Albany,
Auckland 1310, New Zealand (a division of Pearson New Zealand Ltd)
Penguin Books (South Africa) (Pty) Ltd, 24 Sturdee Avenue,
Rosebank 2196, South Africa

Penguin Books Ltd, Registered Offices: 80 Strand, London WC2R 0RL, England

www.penguin.com

This revised translation of *The Republic* first published in Penguin Classics 1987
This translation of *The Symposium* first published in Penguin Classics 1999
These extracts published in Penguin Books 2005

7

The Republic translation copyright © H. D. P. Lee, 1987
The Symposium translation copyright © Christopher Gill, 1999
All rights reserved

Taken from the Penguin Classics edition of *The Symposium*, translated with an
introduction by Christopher Gill and *The Republic*, translated with an
introduction by Desmond Lee

Set by Rowland Phototypesetting Ltd, Bury St Edmunds, Suffolk
Printed in England by Clays Ltd, St Ives plc

ISBN-13: 978–0–14–102384–7

www.greenpenguin.co.uk

Penguin Books is committed to a sustainable future
for our business, our readers and our planet.
The book in your hands is made from paper
certified by the Forest Stewardship Council.

Contents

The Symposium

APOLLODORUS: In fact, I'm well prepared to answer your question. As it happens, the other day I was going to the city from my home in Phalerum, and someone I know spotted me from behind and called me from a distance. He said (with playful urgency):

'Hey, the man from Phalerum! You! Apollodorus, won't you wait?'

I stopped and waited.

He said, 'Apollodorus, I've just been looking for you to get the full story of the party at Agathon's, when Socrates, Alcibiades and the rest were there for dinner: what did they say in their speeches on love? I had a report from someone who got it from Philip's son, Phoenix; but he said you knew about it too. He wasn't able to give an exact report. Please give me your account. Socrates is your friend, and no one has a better right to report his conversations than you. But before you do,' he added, 'tell me this: were you at this party yourself or not?'

'It certainly wasn't an exact report you were given,' I replied, 'if you think this party was recent enough for me to be there.'

'Yes, I did think that,' he said.

'How could you think that, Glaucon? Don't you know that it's many years since Agathon stopped living in

Athens, but it's not yet three years since I started to spend my time with Socrates and made it my job to find out what he says and does every day? Before then, I used to run around aimlessly. I thought I was doing something important, but really I was in the most pathetic state – just like you now! – thinking that philosophy was the last thing I should be doing.'

'Don't make fun of me,' he said; 'just tell me when this party took place.'

'When you and I were still children,' I said, 'and Agathon won the prize with his first tragedy. It was the day after he and his chorus held a sacrificial feast to celebrate their victory.'

'So it really was a long time ago,' he said. 'Who gave you your report; was it Socrates himself?'

'Certainly not!' I said. 'It was the same person who told Phoenix, someone called Aristodemus from Cydathenaeum, a little man who always went around barefoot. He was at the party because he was, I think, one of the people most in love with Socrates at that time. But, of course, I checked with Socrates afterwards some of the points he told me, and he confirmed Aristodemus' account.'

'Come on,' he said, 'why don't you repeat this to me now? After all, walking on the road to the city gives us a good chance to talk and listen as we go along.'

So as we walked along this is what we talked about, and that's why, as I said at the start, I'm well prepared. If I need to go through it for you as well, that's what I must do. In fact, whenever I discuss philosophy or listen to others doing so, I enjoy it enormously, quite apart from thinking it's doing me good. But when I hear other kinds of discussion, especially the talk of rich businessmen like you, I get bored and feel sorry for you and your friends, because you think you're doing something important, when you're not. Perhaps you regard me as a failure, and I think you're right. But I don't *think* you're a failure, I *know* you are.

COMPANION: You're always the same, Apollodorus. You're always running down yourself and other people. You seem to believe that simply everyone is in a sad state except Socrates, beginning with yourself. How you ever got the nickname of 'the softy', I don't know. In your conversation, you're always just the same as you are now, savage in your attacks on yourself and everyone – except Socrates.

APOLLODORUS: Well, my dear friend, it's quite obvious, is it, that if I take this view about myself and you, I'm raving mad?

COMPANION: It's not worth quarrelling about this now, Apollodorus. Please, just do what I asked you, and tell me how the speeches went.

APOLLODORUS: All right, they went something like this – but it would be better if I try to tell the story from the beginning, just as Aristodemus did.

He said that he met Socrates, who'd just had a bath and put on sandals – things he hardly ever did. He asked Socrates where he was going looking so smart.

Socrates replied, 'To dinner with Agathon. Yesterday I stayed away from his victory celebrations, avoiding the crowd; but I promised to join him today. That's why I've smartened myself up, so that I can look good when

I go to the home of a good-looking man. But what about you?' he asked. 'How would you feel about coming to dinner without an invitation?'

'I'll do whatever you say,' Aristodemus replied.

'Come with me, then,' Socrates said, 'so we can prove the proverb wrong, and make it say: "Good men go uninvited to *good* men's banquets". Homer, after all, doesn't just prove the proverb wrong but comes close to treating it with contempt. His Agamemnon is an exceptionally good fighter, while Menelaus is a "soft spearman". But when Agamemnon sacrifices and holds a feast, he makes Menelaus, the inferior man, go uninvited to the banquet of a better man.'

Aristodemus replied to this, 'But I'm afraid that I will also match Homer's description rather than yours, Socrates, and be the inferior man who goes uninvited to the banquet of a clever one. If you take me along, think about what excuse you'll give; I won't admit I've come uninvited, I'll say you've invited me.'

'"The two of us going together on our way"', he said, 'will work out what to say. Come on, then.'

After this conversation, Aristodemus said, they went off. But Socrates fell into his own private thoughts and kept dropping behind as they went along. When Aristodemus stopped too, Socrates told him to go ahead. When Aristodemus reached Agathon's house, he found the door open, and was caught in a ridiculous situation. One of the household slaves met him right away and took him to the room where the others were lying on their couches; and he found them just about to have dinner. As soon as Agathon saw him, he said, 'Aristodemus! You've come at just the right time to have dinner with us. If you've come for any other reason, put it off. I looked for you yesterday to invite you, but couldn't find you. But what about Socrates – why haven't you brought him along?'

When he turned round (Aristodemus said), he saw Socrates wasn't following after all. He explained that Socrates had brought *him* along, and that he was coming to dinner at Socrates' invitation.

'I'm very glad you are,' Agathon said. 'But where is he?'

'He was behind me just now. I can't think where he must be.'

'Go and look, slave,' Agathon said, 'and bring Socrates here. And you, Aristodemus, share Eryximachus' couch.'

A slave washed Aristodemus' hands and feet, so he could lie down. One of the other slaves came and said, 'Socrates is here; he's retreated into your neighbour's porch and is standing there, and won't come in, although I've asked him to.'

'That's odd,' Agathon said. 'Go on asking him in and don't leave him alone.'

'No,' Aristodemus said; 'leave him. This is one of his habits. Sometimes he goes off and stands still wherever he happens to be. He'll come soon, I'm sure. Don't bother him, leave him alone.'

'Well, if you think so, that's what we must do,' Agathon said. 'Now, slaves, serve dinner to the rest of us. You generally serve whatever you like, when nobody is supervising you – and I've never done that. On this occasion, treat me as your guest for dinner as well as the others, and look after us in a way that will win our compliments.'

So they started having dinner, but Socrates still didn't come in. Agathon kept on saying they should send for Socrates, but Aristodemus wouldn't let him. In fact, Socrates came quite soon (he hadn't taken too long doing what he usually did), when they were about half-way through dinner. Then Agathon, who happened to be lying on his own on the bottom couch, said, 'Come and lie down beside me, Socrates, so that, by contact with you, I can share the piece of wisdom that came to you in the porch. It's clear you found what you were looking for and have it now; otherwise you wouldn't have stopped.'

Socrates sat down and said, 'How splendid it would be, Agathon, if wisdom was the sort of thing that could flow from the fuller to the emptier of us when we touch each other, like water, which flows through a piece of wool from a fuller cup to an emptier one. If wisdom is really like that, I regard it as a great privilege to share your couch. I expect to be filled up from your rich supply of fine wisdom. My wisdom is surely inferior – or rather, questionable in its significance, like a dream – but yours is brilliant and has great potential for growth. Look at the way it has blazed out so fiercely while you're still young; it was on display the other day, with more than thirty thousand Greeks there to see it.'

'You're treating me with contempt,' Agathon said. 'We'll argue for our rival claims to wisdom a bit later, and Dionysus will be our judge. But turn your attention to dinner first.'

After this, Aristodemus said, Socrates lay down and

had dinner with the rest. They then poured libations, sang a hymn, and performed all the other customary rituals, and turned to drinking. Pausanias took the initiative, saying something like this: 'Well, gentlemen, what's the most undemanding way to do our drinking? I can tell you that I'm in a really bad state from yesterday's drinking and need a rest. I think that's true of many of you, as you were there yesterday – so think about how to do our drinking in the most undemanding way.'

Aristophanes said, 'You're right, Pausanias, in saying we should cut down the demands we make on ourselves in our drinking. I'm one of those who were thoroughly sodden yesterday.'

After this, Eryximachus, the son of Acumenus, said, 'I agree with you. But there's still one more person I need to hear from, to find out what stamina he has for drinking, and that's Agathon.'

'I've got absolutely no stamina either,' he said.

'It's a stroke of luck for us – I mean, for Aristodemus, Phaedrus and the rest – that you who've got the strongest heads for drinking have given up. We're never up to it. Of course, I don't count Socrates: he can drink or not drink, so it'll suit him whatever we do. Well, since nobody here seems keen on drinking a lot, perhaps you won't find it so tiresome if I state the real facts about getting drunk. It has become clear from my medical experience that drunkenness is harmful for human beings. So if I had my way I wouldn't want to go too far in drinking and I wouldn't advise anyone else to do so, especially when you've still got a hangover from the night before.'

Phaedrus of Myrrhinus spoke up at this point: 'I usually follow your advice, especially where medicine is concerned. The rest of us here will do so too, if they're sensible.'

At this, they all agreed not to make the present occasion a real drinking-session, but just to drink as much as was pleasant.

'Well then,' said Eryximachus, 'now that it's agreed that each of us should drink as much as he wants, without any kind of compulsion, my next proposal is that we should send away the flute-girl who's just come in, and let her play for herself, or for the women in their part of the house, if she prefers, and that we should spend the evening in conversation. Also, if you're willing, I'd like to propose a topic for discussion.'

They all agreed and told him to make his proposal. Eryximachus said, 'I want to begin by quoting the *Melanippe* of Euripides: "Not mine the story" that I'm going to tell, but that of Phaedrus here. He often makes this complaint: "Isn't it terrible, Eryximachus," he says, "that the poets have composed hymns and paeans to other gods, but none of them has ever composed a eulogy of Love, though he is such an ancient and important god. If you look at our best sophists (for instance, the excellent Prodicus), they write eulogies in prose to Heracles and the rest. Perhaps that's not so very surprising; but I once found a book by a clever writer in which salt gets amazing praise for its beneficial properties, and you can find encomia to many other such things. It's terrible that people have given serious attention to subjects like that, but nobody to this day has yet had the courage to sing the praises of Love as he deserves. Such a great god and so neglected!'' I think Phaedrus is quite right on this point. I'd like to please him by making a contribution to this project; also this seems a good occasion for those of us here to celebrate the god. If you agree, we won't need anything to occupy us but discussion. I propose that each of us should make the finest speech he can in praise of Love, and then pass the topic on to the one on his right. Phaedrus should start, because he is in the top position, and is also the originator of the topic.'

'Nobody will vote against you, Eryximachus,' Socrates said. 'I certainly couldn't refuse, since the subject of love is the only one I claim to understand. Nor could Agathon and Pausanias; nor could Aristophanes, whose whole occupation is centred on Dionysus and Aphrodite; nor could anyone else I see here. Of course, this arrangement isn't fair on those of us whose positions come last. But if the first comers say all that is required and do it well, that will satisfy us. Good luck to Phaedrus as he starts off and makes his eulogy of Love!'

All the rest agreed with this and told Phaedrus to do as Socrates said. Of course, Aristodemus didn't remember all that each speaker said and I don't remember all he said. But I'll tell you the speeches of the people he remembered best and that I thought most important.

As I say, Aristodemus told me that Phaedrus spoke first, starting along these lines: saying that Love was regarded by humans and gods as a great and awesome god for many reasons, especially his origin.

'The god', he said, 'is held in honour because he is one of the most ancient, as is proved by this fact: Love has no parents and none are ascribed to him by prose writers or poets. Hesiod says that first Chaos came into existence,

> and then
> Broad-breasted Earth, a secure seat for everything for ever,
> And Love.

Acusilaus agrees with Hesiod, saying that after Chaos two things came into existence, Earth and Love. On his origin, Parmenides says that "the very first god she devised was Love". So Love's great antiquity is widely accepted.

'Because of his antiquity, he is the source of our greatest benefits. I would claim that there is no greater benefit for a young man than a good lover and none greater for a lover than a good boyfriend. Neither family bonds nor public status nor wealth nor anything else is as effective as love in implanting something which gives lifelong guidance to those who are to lead good lives. What is this? A sense of shame at acting disgracefully and pride in acting well. Without these no individual or city can achieve anything great or fine.

'Take the case of a man in love who is caught acting disgracefully or undergoing something disgraceful because he fails to defend himself out of cowardice. I think it would cause him more pain to be seen in this situation by his boyfriend than by his father, his friends or anyone else. We see the same thing in the case of the boyfriend: he feels most ashamed in front of his lovers when he is caught in some disgraceful situation. If there was any mechanism for producing a city or army consisting of lovers and boyfriends, there could be no better form of social organization than this: they would hold back from anything disgraceful and compete for honour in each other's eyes. If even small numbers of such men fought side by side, they could defeat virtually the whole human race. The last person a lover could bear to be seen by, when leaving his place in the battle-line or abandoning his weapons, is his boyfriend; instead, he'd prefer to die many times. As for abandoning his boyfriend or failing to help him in danger – no one is such a coward that he could not be inspired into courage by love and made the equal of someone who's naturally very brave. When Homer speaks about a god "breathing might" into some of his heroes, this is just the effect that love has on lovers.

'Besides, it's only lovers who are willing to die for someone else; and this is true of women as well as men. The Greeks have adequate proof of this fact in Pelias' daughter Alcestis, who was the only one willing to die for her husband, though his father and mother were still living. Acting out of love, she showed so much more affectionate concern than they did that she made them look like strangers to their son, and relatives only in name. The gods, as well as human beings, saw this as a very fine act. Although many people have performed many fine acts, and although the gods have granted to only a handful of these the privilege of releasing their life again from Hades, they released her life, in admiration at her act. This shows how much even the gods value the commitment and courage that come from love.

'But they sent Orpheus, the son of Oeagrus, empty handed from Hades; they showed him only a phantom of the wife he'd come to fetch and didn't give him the woman herself. They thought he was soft (he was only a musician) because he didn't have the courage to die for his love like Alcestis, but found a way of entering Hades while still alive. They punished him for this, and made him die at the hands of women.

'By contrast, they honoured Achilles, the son of Thetis, and sent him off to the islands of the blessed. He learnt from his mother that if he killed Hector he would then die himself, but that if he didn't he would go home and die in his old age. He had the courage to choose to act on behalf of his lover by avenging him: he not only died *for* him but also died *as well as* him, since Patroclus was already dead. This won special admiration and exceptional honours from the gods, because it showed how much he valued his lover. Aeschylus talks nonsense when he says that Achilles was Patroclus' lover: he was more beautiful than Patroclus (indeed, he was the most beautiful of all the heroes), and was still beardless, as well as much younger than Patroclus, as Homer tells us. Although the gods certainly give special honour to the courage that comes from love, they show still greater amazement and admiration, and respond more generously, when a boyfriend shows affectionate concern towards his lover than when a lover does towards his boyfriend. A lover is more god-like than a boyfriend because he is divinely inspired. That's why they gave higher honour to Achilles than Alcestis, and sent him to the islands of the blessed.

'That's why I say Love is the most ancient of the gods, the most honoured, and the most effective in enabling human beings to acquire courage and happiness, both in life and death.'

Phaedrus' speech went rather like that, according to Aristodemus. After Phaedrus, there were some others which Aristodemus couldn't remember very well; so he missed them out and went on to report Pausanias' speech. Pausanias said, 'I don't think our project has been specified properly, Phaedrus, in that we've been told simply to praise Love. If Love were a single thing, this would be fine, but in fact it isn't; and since it isn't, it's better to define in advance which type we should praise. I'll try and put things right by stating first which Love we should praise, then giving the god the praise he deserves.

'We all know that Aphrodite is inseparable from Love. If there was a single Aphrodite, there would be a single Love; but since there are two kinds of Aphrodite, there must also be two Loves. And surely there *are* two kinds of Aphrodite? One of these is older and is the daughter of Uranus, though she has no mother: we call her Uranian or Heavenly Aphrodite. The younger one is the daughter of Zeus and Dione: we call her Pandemic or Common Aphrodite. So it follows that each type of Love should have the same name as the goddess whose partner he is, and be called Heavenly or Common too. Of course, all gods should receive praise, but we must try and distinguish between the functions of these two gods.

'Every activity in itself is neither right nor wrong. Take our present activity: we could be drinking or singing or discussing. None of these is right in itself; the character of the activity depends on the way it is done. If it is done rightly and properly, it is right; if it is not done properly, it is wrong. So not every type of loving and Love is right and deserves to be praised, but only the type that motivates us to love rightly.

'Common Love is genuinely "common" and undiscriminating in its effects; this is the kind of love that inferior people feel. People like this are attracted to women as much as boys, and to bodies rather than minds. They are attracted to partners with the least possible intelligence, because their sole aim is to get what they want, and they don't care whether they do this rightly or not. So the effect of love on them is that they act without discrimination: it is all the same to them whether they behave well or not. The reason is that their love derives from the goddess who is much younger than the other, and who, because of her origin, is partly female and partly male in character.

'The other love derives from the Heavenly goddess, who has nothing of the female in her but only maleness; so this love is directed at boys. This goddess is also older, and so avoids abusive violence. That's why those inspired with this love are drawn towards the male, feeling affection for what is naturally more vigorous and intelligent. You can also distinguish, within the general class of those attracted to boys, the ones who are motivated purely by the heavenly type of love. These are attracted to boys only when they start to have developed intelligence, and this happens around the time that they begin to grow a beard. I think that those who begin love-affairs at this point show their readiness to spend their whole lives together and to lead a fully shared life. They do not plan to trick the boy, catching him while he is still young and foolish, and then leaving with a laugh, running off to someone else.

'There should even be a law against affairs with young boys, to prevent great effort being spent on something whose outcome is unclear. In the case of young boys, it is unclear whether they will end up good or bad in mind or body. Good men make this rule for themselves and are glad to do so. The followers of Common Love should be forced to adopt the same kind of rule, just as we forcibly prevent them, as far as we can, from having affairs with free-born women. These are the men who bring censure on love, so that some people go so far as to say that it is wrong to gratify a lover at all. People say this because they have in view the inappropriate and unjust behaviour of this type of men; surely, there is no action which would rightly be criticized if it were done in an orderly way and in line with the normal conventions.

'The conventions governing love-affairs in other cities are easy to grasp since they have been defined in straight-forward terms. But here and in Sparta they are complex. In Elis and Boeotia, and wherever people are poor at speaking, the rule has been laid down straightforwardly that it is right to gratify lovers, and no one, young or old, would say that it is wrong. No doubt, this is to save them the trouble of trying to win over young men by persuasion, bearing in mind that they're incompetent speakers. But in much of Ionia and elsewhere in the Persian Empire the rule is that love-affairs are wrong. In

Persia, it is because of their tyrannical government that they condemn them, as well as intellectual and athletic activities. No doubt, it doesn't suit their government that their subjects should have big ideas or develop strong friendships and personal bonds, which are promoted by all these activities, especially by love. In Athens the tyrants found this out by their own experience: it was Aristogiton's love and the strength of Harmodius' reciprocal affection that brought their dominance to an end. So where there is a general rule that it is wrong to gratify lovers, this can be attributed to the defects of those who make this rule: the government's lust for rule and the subjects' cowardice. Where the rule is that it is straightforwardly right, this is because of the mental sluggishness of the rule-makers.

'Here in Athens our conventions are much better than those; but, as I've said, they are not easy to understand. It is said to be better to love openly than secretly, especially if you love boys of social distinction and good character, even if they are not particularly good looking. Also the lover receives an extraordinary amount of encouragement from everyone, which suggests that he isn't doing anything disgraceful; it is regarded as a fine thing to catch the boy you want and disgraceful to fail. When the lover is trying to catch the boy, convention allows him to win praise for doing extraordinary things. If he dared to do these things with any other aim and objective, his reward would be massive disapproval.

'Imagine that someone who wanted to get money from a person, or political office or some other position of influence, was prepared to behave as lovers do towards the boys they love. Imagine that he went down on his knees as a suppliant, begging for what he wanted, and swore oaths, and spent all night on someone's doorstep, and was prepared to undergo the kind of slavery that no slave would put up with. He would be held back from behaving like this by friends and enemies alike; his enemies would criticize him for humiliating himself to get what he wanted, while his friends would tell him to stop and be ashamed of what he'd done. But when a lover does all these things, he is indulged and allowed by convention to escape criticism, implying that his objective is wholly admirable. Most remarkable of all, it is widely supposed that the only person forgiven by the gods for failing to keep an oath is the lover. A lover's oath, they say, is no oath at all. So, according to our convention, gods as well as humans allow lovers every kind of indulgence. From this standpoint, you would think that in this city it is regarded as wholly admirable to be a lover and to respond affectionately to one's lovers.

'On the other hand, when boys attract lovers, their fathers put attendants in charge of them, with specific instructions not to let the boys have conversations with their lovers. The boys' friends and peer group call them names if they see anything like this going on, and older people don't stop the name-calling or tell them off for saying these things. When you look at this, you would think, by contrast, that love-affairs were regarded as wholly wrong here.

'The position, I think, is this. The matter is not straight-forward; and, as I said before, a love-affair in itself is neither right nor wrong but right when it is conducted rightly and wrong when conducted wrongly. It is wrong to gratify a bad man in a bad way, and right to gratify a good man in the right way. A bad man, in this connection, is the lover of the common type, who loves the body rather than the mind. He is not constant, because he loves something that is not constant: as soon as the bloom of the body fades, which is what attracted him, "he flies away and is gone", bringing disgrace on all he said and promised. But the man who loves goodness of character is constant throughout his life, since he has become united with something constant.

'The aim of our practice is to test lovers thoroughly and in the right way, to ensure that boys gratify one type but keep away from the other. That is why, at the same time, we encourage lovers to chase boys and encourage boys to run away from lovers. It's a kind of competition to test which type the lover belongs to and which type the boy belongs to. This explains why it's considered wrong to be caught quickly: this is to ensure that time intervenes, which is thought to be a good way of testing most things. It also explains why it is considered wrong to be caught by a lover's money or political power. In such cases, the boy is either frightened into submission by ill-treatment or enjoys the benefits of money or political success and fails to look down on this sort of thing. None of these things are thought to be stable or permanent, apart from the fact that no genuine affection can be based on them.

'Only one way remains, according to our rules, in which it is right for a boy to gratify his lover. I said earlier that the lover's willingness to undergo every kind of slavery isn't humiliating or reprehensible. Similarly, according to our rules, there's only one remaining type of voluntary slavery that isn't reprehensible: the type which aims to produce virtue. Our view is that if someone is willing to put himself at someone else's service in the belief that the other person will help him improve in wisdom or some other aspect of virtue, this willing slavery isn't wrong or humiliating.

'These two rules must be combined (the one governing the love of boys and the one governing the love of wisdom and other kinds of virtue), to create the conditions in which it is right for a boy to gratify his lover. These conditions are realized when lover and boyfriend come together, each observing the appropriate rule: that the lover is justified in any service he performs for the boyfriend who gratifies him, and that the boyfriend is justified in any favour he does for someone who is making him wise and good. Also the lover must be able to develop the boyfriend's understanding and virtue in general, and the boyfriend must want to acquire education and wisdom in general. When all these conditions are met, then and then alone it is right for a boyfriend to gratify his lover, but not otherwise.

'In this case, there's nothing wrong with being deceived; but, in every other case, love is wrong, whether or not you are deceived. Suppose that a boy thinks his lover is rich and gratifies him in the hope of making money; if the lover turns out to be poor and the boy doesn't get any money, what he does is still wrong. This kind of boy has shown something about his character:

that he would do any service for anyone to make money, and that is not right. On the same basis, suppose a boy thinks that his lover is a good man and gratifies him in the hope of becoming better through the lover's friendship. If the lover turns out to be a bad person, quite lacking in virtue, there's no disgrace in being deceived in this way. This kind of boy has also shown something about his character: that he's keen to do anything for anybody to gain virtue and become better, and there's no motive more admirable than this. So it's absolutely right to gratify a lover in the hope of gaining virtue. This is the heavenly love that belongs to the Heavenly goddess and is a source of great value to the city and to individuals, because it forces the lover to pay attention to his own virtue and the boyfriend to do the same. All other forms of love derive from the other Love, the Common one.

'This is my contribution on Love, Phaedrus,' he said; 'it's as good as I can manage on the spur of the moment.'

When Pausanias came to a pause (I have learnt this kind of word-play from the experts), Aristodemus said, it was Aristophanes' turn to speak. But, as it happened, he was having an attack of hiccups, from overeating or some other cause, and couldn't speak. He said to Eryximachus (the doctor was lying on the couch below his), 'You're the right person either to put a stop to my hiccups or to speak instead of me until they're over.' Eryximachus replied, 'I'll do both. I'll take your place and you take mine when your hiccups are over. While I'm speaking, your hiccups might stop if you hold your breath for a long time; if they don't, gargle with some water. If they're really persistent, get something to tickle your nose with, and make yourself sneeze. If you do this once or twice, they'll stop, however persistent they are.'

'Start your speech as soon as you can,' said Aristophanes, 'and I'll do this.'

Eryximachus said, 'This is what I think: Pausanias started his speech well but did not carry it through to a proper conclusion, so I should try to complete his line of argument. I think he drew a good distinction in saying there are two kinds of Love. But Love is not only expressed in the emotional responses of human beings to beautiful people, but in many other types of response as well: in the bodily responses of every kind of animal, in plants growing in the earth, in virtually everything that exists. I feel sure it's from medicine, my own area of expertise, that I've realized how great and wonderful a god Love is, and how his power extends to all aspects of human and divine life.

'I'll begin with medicine, to give pride of place to this form of expertise. It's inherent in the nature of bodies that they manifest these two kinds of love. It's generally agreed that bodily health and disease are different states and dissimilar from each other. When things are dissimilar, the objects of their desire and love are dissimilar. Therefore, love is different in the case of a healthy and a diseased body. Pausanias just said that it's right to gratify good people but wrong to gratify self-indulgent ones. It's just the same with the body: in the case of each body, it is right to gratify the good parts and you should do this (and that's what it means to practise medicine); but it's wrong to gratify the bad and diseased parts and you should deprive them of satisfaction if you're going to be an expert doctor.

'Medicine, in essence, is knowledge of the forms of bodily love as regards filling and emptying. The person who is most of all a doctor can distinguish, within these processes, between right and wrong love. The good practitioner can bring about changes, so that the body acquires one type of love instead of the other; he knows how to implant one type of love, when it isn't there but should be, and to remove the other type of love that is there. He should be able to take the most antagonistic elements in the body and create friendship and love between them. The most antagonistic elements are opposites such as cold and hot, bitter and sweet, dry and wet, and so on. The one who discovered how to implant love and concord between these was our ancestor Asclepius (that's what we're told by poets like those here, and I believe them) and that's how he established the art of medicine.

'Medicine, as I say, is wholly governed by this god, and so are athletics and agriculture; and it's clear to anyone who thinks about it for a moment that the same point applies to music. This is perhaps what Heraclitus has in mind, though he doesn't express it very well. He says about unity that "by diverging, it agrees with itself . . . like the harmony of a bow or a lyre". It is quite absurd to say that a harmony diverges from itself or that it exists while its components are still divergent. But perhaps what he had in mind was that musical expertise creates harmony by replacing a previous divergence between high and low notes with agreement. Surely there can be no harmony between high and low while they are still divergent. Harmony is concord, and concord is a kind of agreement; but agreement cannot be created from divergent things while they are still divergent, and harmony cannot be created unless divergent things agree. Similarly, rhythm is created by replacing a previous divergence between fast and slow tempo with agreement. Just as medicine creates agreement in one area, music creates it in another, by implanting love and concord between the elements involved; music, in its turn, is knowledge of the forms of love in connection with harmony and rhythm.

'In the structure of harmony and rhythm, considered in itself, it's not difficult to recognize the workings of love; and so the twofold character of love does not show itself here. But when it's a question of using rhythm and harmony to produce an effect on people, either by making up music (what they call "composition") or by making proper use of the tunes and verses composed (which is called "education"), difficulties arise and a good practitioner is needed. Here the same principle again holds good: you should gratify and promote the love of well-ordered people, or people who are not yet well ordered but may in this way improve. This love is the good and heavenly one, the love of the Heavenly Muse. But the common love is that of the Muse Polymnia; when this type of love is applied, it must be with caution, to ensure that the recipient enjoys the pleasure it provides without being made self-indulgent. Similarly, in my area of expertise, a key part of the job lies in the correct handling of the desires met by the art of cookery, to ensure that people enjoy this pleasure without getting ill. So in music, medicine, and in every other sphere, both human and divine, as far as we can, we must pay careful attention to these two kinds of love, because both kinds are there.

'The character of the seasons is also determined by these two kinds of love. When those elements I mentioned before (hot and cold, dry and wet) are influenced by the well-ordered Love, they are in harmony with each other and achieve a temperate mixture. Their arrival brings good harvests and health to humans and other animals and plants, and causes no damage. But when the lawless and violent Love dominates the seasons, they cause great destruction and damage. These conditions tend to produce epidemics and other abnormal diseases for beasts and plants. Frost, hail and blight are the result of the mutually aggressive competition and disorder that is the effect of this kind of love. So what we call astronomy is the knowledge of the workings of love, as these affect the movements of the stars and the seasons of the year.

'Also, all types of sacrifice and the whole sphere of divination (these are the ways in which gods and humans communicate with each other) are wholly directed at maintaining one kind of love and curing the other. Every kind of impiety towards one's parents (living or dead) or the gods tends to occur when people fail to gratify, respect or give pride of place in every action to the well-ordered Love, but do so to the other one. Prophecy has been given the job of keeping an eye on those whose love is the wrong kind and curing this. It also has the job of producing friendship between gods and humans by understanding how the operations of love in human life affect right behaviour and piety.

'So Love as a whole has great and mighty – or rather total – power, when you put all this together. But it is the Love whose nature is expressed in good actions, marked by self-control and justice, at the human and divine level that has the greatest power and is the source of all our happiness. It enables us to associate, and be friends, with each other and with the gods, our superiors.

'It may be that my eulogy of Love has missed out a good deal, but if so this was not intentional. If I have left anything out, it's up to you, Aristophanes, to fill in the gaps. Or, if you have in mind a different kind of eulogy of the god, do carry on, now that your hiccups have stopped.'

Now that it was Aristophanes' turn (Aristodemus reported), he said: 'Yes, they've stopped all right, but not until I applied the sneeze-treatment to them. It makes me wonder whether it is the "well-ordered" part of my body that wants the kind of noises and tickles that make up a sneeze. At any rate, the hiccups stopped right away when I applied the sneeze.'

'My dear Aristophanes,' Eryximachus said, 'be careful what you're doing. By joking before you start to speak, you're making me watch out for jokes in your speech too, when otherwise you could give your speech without interference.'

'You're right, Eryximachus,' Aristophanes said, 'and I withdraw what I said. But, if you're watching out in my speech, don't think I'm afraid of saying something funny

– that would be pure profit and typical of my Muse – but of saying something ludicrous.'

Eryximachus said, 'You think you can take a shot at me and run away! Well, take care; you'll have to answer for what you say. But even so, if I decide to, I'll let you off.'

'Actually, Eryximachus,' Aristophanes said, 'I do intend to take a different approach from the one taken by you and Pausanias in your speeches. I think people have wholly failed to recognize the power of Love; if they'd grasped this, they'd have built the greatest temples and altars for him, and made the greatest sacrifices. In fact, none of this is done for him, though he deserves it most of all. He loves human beings more than any other god; he is their helper and the doctor of those sicknesses whose cure constitutes the greatest happiness for the human race. I shall try to explain his power to you, and you will teach this to others.

'First of all, you must learn about human nature, and what has happened to it. Long ago, our nature was not the same as it is now but quite different. For one thing, there were three human genders, not just the present two, male and female. There was also a third one, a combination of these two; now its name survives, although the gender has vanished. Then "androgynous" was a distinct gender as well as a name, combining male and female; now nothing is left but the name, which is used as an insult.

'For another thing, the shape of each human being was a rounded whole, with back and sides forming a circle. Each one had four hands and the same number of legs, and two identical faces on a circular neck. They had one head for both the faces, which were turned in opposite directions, four ears, two sets of genitals, and everything else was as you would imagine from what I've said so far. They moved around upright as we do now, in either direction, as they wanted. When they set off to run fast, they supported themselves on all their eight limbs, and moved quickly round and round, like tumblers who do cartwheels by keeping their legs straight as they go round and round.

'The reason why there were these three genders, and why they were as described, is that the parent of the male gender was originally the sun, that of the female gender the earth, that of the combined gender the moon, because the moon is a combination of sun and earth. They were round, and so was the way they moved, because they took after their parents. They were terrible in their strength and vigour; they had great ambitions and made an attack on the gods. The story told by Homer about Ephialtes and Otus, how they tried to climb up to heaven to attack the gods, really refers to them. Zeus and the other gods discussed what to do to them and couldn't decide. The gods didn't see how they could kill them, wiping out the human race with thunderbolts as they'd done with the giants; if they did that, the honours and sacrifices the gods received from them would disappear. But they couldn't let them go on behaving outrageously. After much hard thought, Zeus had an idea: "I think I have a plan by which human beings could still exist but be too weak to carry on their wild behaviour. I shall now cut each of them into two; they will be weaker and also more useful to us because there will be more of them. They will walk around upright on two legs. If we think they're still acting outrageously, and they won't settle down, I'll cut them in half again so that they move around hopping on one leg."

'After saying this, Zeus cut humans into two, as people cut sorb-apples in half before they preserve them or as they cut hard-boiled eggs with hairs. As he cut each one, he told Apollo to turn the face and the half-neck attached to it towards the gash, so that humans would see their own wound and be more orderly; Zeus also told him to heal the other wounds. Apollo turned round the face; he pulled the skin from all around the body towards what's now called the stomach (like a purse being pulled tight with a draw-string), and finished it off by making one opening in the middle of the stomach, which we call the navel. He also smoothed off the other numerous wrinkles, and shaped the chest with the kind of tool used by shoemakers when they smooth the wrinkles of leather on the last. But he left a few on the stomach round the navel, to remind them of what had happened to them long ago.

'Since their original nature had been cut in two, each one longed for its own other half and stayed with it. They threw their arms round each other, weaving themselves together, wanting to form a single living thing. So they died from hunger and from general inactivity, because they didn't want to do anything apart from each other. Whenever one of the halves died and one was left, the one that was left looked for another and wove itself together with that. Sometimes the one it met was half of a whole woman (the half we now call a "woman"), sometimes half a whole man. In any case, they kept on dying in this way.

'Zeus took pity on them and came up with another plan: he moved their genitals round to the front; until then, they had genitals on the back of their bodies, and sexual reproduction occurred not with each other but on the earth, as in the case of cicadas. So Zeus moved the genitals round to the front and in this way made them reproduce in each other, by means of the male acting inside the female. The aim of this was that, if a man met with a woman and entwined himself with her, they would reproduce and the human race would be continued. Also, if two males came together, they would at least have the satisfaction of sexual intercourse, and then relax, turn to their work, and think about the other things in their life.

'That's how, long ago, the innate desire of human beings for each other started. It draws the two halves of our original nature back together and tries to make one out of two and to heal the wound in human nature. Each of us is a matching half of a human being, because we've been cut in half like flatfish, making two out of one, and each of us is looking for his own matching half. Those men who are cut from the combined gender (the androgynous, as it was called then) are attracted to women, and many adulterers are from this group. Similarly, the women who are attracted to men and become adulteresses come from this group. Those women who are cut from the female gender are not at all interested in men, but are drawn much more towards women; female homosexuals come from this group.

'Those who are cut from the male gender go for males. While they are boys, because they are slices of the male gender, they are attracted to men and enjoy sleeping with men and being embraced by them. These are the best of their generation, both as boys and young men, because they are naturally the bravest. Some people say that they are shameless, but that isn't true. It's not out of shamelessness that they do this but because they are bold, brave and masculine, and welcome the same qualities in others. Here is clear evidence of this: men like this are the only ones who, when grown up, end up as politicians. When they become men, they're sexually attracted by boys; they have no natural interest in getting married and having children, although they are forced to do this by convention. They are quite satisfied by spending their lives together and not getting married. In short, such people become lovers of boys and boys who love their male lovers, always welcoming their shared natural character.

'When a lover of boys, or any other type of person, meets that very person who is his other half, he is overwhelmed, to an amazing extent, with affection, concern and love. The two don't want to spend any time apart from each other. These are people who live out whole lifetimes together, but still couldn't say what it is they want from each other. I mean, no one can think that it's just sexual intercourse they want, and that this is the reason why they find such joy in each other's company and attach such importance to this. It's clear that each of them has some wish in his mind that he can't articulate; instead, like an oracle, he half-grasps what he wants and obscurely hints at it. Imagine that Hephaestus with his tools stood over them while they were lying together and asked: "What is it, humans, that you want from each other?" If they didn't know, imagine that he asked next: "Is this what you desire, to be together so completely that you're never apart from each other night and day? If this is what you desire, I'm prepared to fuse and weld you together, so that the two of you become one. Then the two of you would live a shared life, as long as you live, since you are one person; and when you died, you would have a shared death in Hades, as one person instead of two. But see if this is what you long for, and if achieving this state satisfies you." We know that no one who heard this offer would turn it down and it would become apparent that no one wanted anything else. Everyone would think that what he was hearing now was just what he'd longed for all this time: to come together and be fused with the one he loved and become one instead of two. The reason is that this is our original natural state and we used to be whole creatures: "love" is the name for the desire and pursuit of wholeness.

'Before this, as I say, we were unified; but now, because of our crimes, we have been split up by Zeus just as the Arcadians have been by the Spartans. There's a danger that, if we aren't well ordered in our behaviour towards the gods, we'll be split up further, and go around like figures in bas-relief on gravestones, sawn in half down the nose, like half-dice. So everyone should encourage others to show all due reverence towards the gods, so that we can avoid one outcome and achieve the other, with Love as our leader and general. No one should work against Love, and to get on the wrong side of the gods is to work against Love. If we are friends of the god and have him on our side, we shall do what few people now do – find and become close to the loved ones that are really our own.

'I don't want Eryximachus to think that my speech is just a comedy, directed at Pausanias and Agathon. It may well be that they are among this type and are both halves of the male nature. But what I'm saying applies to all men and all women too: our human race can only achieve happiness if love reaches its conclusion, and each of us finds his loved one and restores his original nature. If this is the ideal, under present circumstances what comes closest to it must be the best: that is to find a loved one who naturally fits your own character. If we want to praise the god who is responsible for this, we would rightly praise Love. In present circumstances, he does the best for us that can be done, leading us towards what is naturally close to us. He also holds out to us the greatest hopes for the future: that if we show reverence towards the gods, he will restore us to our original nature, healing us and so giving us perfect happiness.

'Well, Eryximachus, this is my speech about love, a rather different one from yours. As I asked you, don't treat my speech as a comedy. Let's go on and hear what each of the remaining speakers has to say – or rather the two of them, as only Agathon and Socrates are left.'

'I'll do as you say,' Eryximachus said, 'and in any

case I much enjoyed your speech. If I didn't know that Socrates and Agathon were experts on the ways of love, I'd be very worried that they might run out of things to say, since we've already had such a wide variety of speeches. But, as things are, I'm quite confident.'

Socrates said, 'That's because you've taken part successfully in our competition. If you were in my position, or rather where I'll be when Agathon too has given a good speech, you'd be very frightened and in just as much of a quandary as I am.'

'You're trying to put a spell on me, Socrates,' Agathon said, 'by making me nervous at the thought that the audience has high expectations of my giving a good speech.'

'But I would have a short memory if I did that, Agathon,' said Socrates. 'I saw the courage and self-confidence you showed when you went out on to the platform with the actors, facing such a huge audience without any embarrassment, before presenting your own work. So I shouldn't expect you to become nervous in front of our small group.'

'But Socrates,' Agathon said, 'I hope you don't think I'm so obsessed with the theatre that I don't realize that, for anyone with any sense, a small number of intelligent people are more alarming than a crowd of unintelligent ones.'

'It would be quite wrong of me, Agathon,' Socrates said, 'to think you could be unsophisticated in any way. I'm well aware that if you found some people you thought were wise, you would pay more attention to them than to the crowd. But I'm afraid we don't fall into that category; after all, we were there and were part of that crowd. But if you found some other wise people, you might feel ashamed if you thought you were doing something wrong in front of them – is that what you mean?'

'That's right,' Agathon replied.

'But wouldn't you feel ashamed if you thought you were doing something wrong in front of the crowd?'

At this point Phaedrus interrupted and said, 'My dear Agathon, if you answer Socrates' questions, he won't care whether we get anywhere with our present project, as long as he's got a partner for discussion, especially someone attractive. I enjoy hearing Socrates engaging in discussion, but I must look after the eulogy of Love and extract from each one of you a speech as your contribution. So when the two of you have made your offering to the god, then you can have your discussion.'

'You're right, Phaedrus,' Agathon said; 'there's no reason for me not to make my speech. Socrates will have plenty of opportunities for discussion another time.

'I want first of all to say how I should speak, then give my speech. I think that all the previous speakers, instead of praising the god, have congratulated human beings on the good things that come to them from the god. Nobody has spoken about the nature of the god himself who has given us these things. There is only one right way of making a eulogy, whatever the topic, and that is to define the nature of the subject of the speech and the nature of that for which he is responsible. So, in the case of Love, the right thing is to praise his nature first, and then his gifts.

'I claim that, though all the gods are happy, Love – if it is proper to say this and does not cause offence – is the happiest, because he is the most beautiful and best. He is the most beautiful for this reason: first of all, Phaedrus, he is the youngest of gods. He himself provides good evidence for this point by fleeing headlong from old age, fast though that is (it comes to us sooner than it should). Love naturally hates old age and keeps his distance from it. He always associates with the young and is one of them; the ancient saying is right, that like always stays close to like. Although I agree with many other things that Phaedrus said, I don't agree that Love is older than Cronus and Iapetus. I claim that he is the youngest of the gods and stays young forever. The things the gods did to each other in ancient times, which Hesiod and Parmenides report, happened (if their reports are true) because of Necessity and not Love. The gods would not have castrated or imprisoned each other or done those many other acts of violence if Love had been among them; there would have been friendship and peace between them, as there is now and has been since Love began to rule among the gods.

'He is young, and sensitive as well as young; but it would take a poet of Homer's quality to bring out how sensitive the god is. Homer describes Delusion as a goddess, and also sensitive; at least her feet are sensitive, as he says:

But her feet are sensitive; to the ground
She never draws close, but walks on the heads of men.

I think Homer gives clear evidence of her sensitivity, in saying that she does not walk on what is hard, but what is soft. We can use the same evidence for Love's sensitivity. He does not walk on the ground, nor on skulls (which are not at all soft), but walks and lives in the softest of all things. He makes his home in the characters and minds of gods and humans; and not in all minds, one after another, but whenever he finds one with a tough character he moves on, and whenever he finds one with a soft character he settles down. Since he is in continual contact with the softest members of the softest type of thing, not just with his feet but with all of him, he must be extremely sensitive.

'So he is very young and sensitive, and is fluid in shape as well. Otherwise, if he was tough, he couldn't envelop someone's mind completely or pass unnoticed at first entry into it and then out of it. Good evidence that he has a well-formed and fluid shape comes from his gracefulness, which is universally accepted as a special feature of Love (gracelessness and Love are always enemies to each other). His beauty of complexion is shown by the fact that he spends his time among flowers. Love does not settle on a body or mind or anything that has no bloom or has lost its bloom; but when he finds somewhere full of bloom and fragrance, there he settles and stays.

'Enough has been said (though still more remains) about the god's beauty; the next topic I must speak about is Love's virtue. The most important point is that Love does no injustice and has none done to him, when dealing with either gods or humans. When Love has anything done to him, it isn't by force (since Love is never forced). When Love does anything, he doesn't use force, since everyone consents to all Love's orders; and whatever is agreed by mutual consent, that is what "laws, the sovereign of the city" define as just.

'As well as justice, Love has the biggest share of moderation. It is generally agreed that moderation is mastery of pleasures and desires, and that no pleasure is stronger than Love. If the pleasures are weaker, they must be mastered by Love and he must be their master; and if Love masters pleasures and desires, he must be exceptionally moderate.

'As for courage, "not even Ares can stand up to" Love. It isn't Ares who captured Love but Love who captured Ares (Love of Aphrodite, as the story goes), and the capturer is master of the captured. Whoever masters the one who is bravest of the others must be the bravest of all.

'I've spoken about the god's justice, moderation and courage; it remains to speak about his wisdom. As far as possible, I must try to treat this fully. First of all – to give honour to my expertise in the way that Eryximachus gave honour to his – the god is so skilled a poet that he makes others into poets. Everyone turns into a poet, "even though a stranger to the Muses before", when he is touched by Love. We may take this as evidence that Love is a good composer in, broadly, every type of artistic production, because you can't give someone else what you don't have or teach someone what you don't know yourself. Certainly, as regards the production of living things, who will deny that it is by Love's skill that all living things come into being and are produced? As for expertise in art or craft, don't we know that whoever is taught by this god ends up being famous and conspicuous, while whoever is untouched by the god is obscure? It was by following where his desire and love led him that Apollo discovered the arts of archery, medicine and prophecy, and this makes Apollo a pupil of Love. In the same way, it makes the Muses pupils of his in music, Hephaestus in metalwork, Athena in weaving and Zeus in steering gods and humans. So the activities of the gods only became organized when Love was born among them – love of beauty, of course, as love cannot be directed at ugliness. Before then, as I said at the start, the gods did many terrible things, we are told, under the rule of Necessity. But once this god was born, all good things came to gods and humans through the love of beauty.

'So it seems to me, Phaedrus, that Love is himself supreme in beauty and excellence and is responsible for similar qualities in others. I feel moved to express this in verse and say that he is the one who makes

> Peace among humankind and windless calm at sea,
> Rest for the winds, and sleep for those distressed.

Love drains us of estrangement and fills us with familiarity, causing us to come together in all shared gatherings like this, and acting as our leader in festival, chorus and sacrifice. He includes mildness and excludes wildness. He is generous of goodwill and ungenerous of ill-will. He is gracious and kindly; gazed on by the wise, admired by the gods; craved by those denied him, treasured by those enjoying him; father of luxury, elegance, delicacy, grace, desire, longing; careful for good people, careless of bad people; in trouble, in terror, in longing, in discourse, he is the best helmsman, marine, comrade, rescuer. For the whole company of gods and humans, most beautiful and best of leaders; every man should follow him singing beautiful hymns of praise, sharing the song he sings to charm the mind of every god and human.

'There's my speech, Phaedrus,' he said, 'my dedication to the god; it combines entertainment with a degree of seriousness, as far as I can manage.'

After Agathon had finished his speech, Aristodemus said, there were shouts of admiration from everyone present, because the young man had spoken in a way that reflected well on himself and on the god. Socrates looked at Eryximachus and said, 'Well, son of Acumenus, do you still think my earlier anxiety was groundless? Wasn't I speaking prophetically when I said just now that Agathon would give an amazing speech and that I would be lost for words?'

'On one point', Eryximachus said, 'you were prophetic, in saying that Agathon would give a good speech; but I don't think you'll be lost for words.'

'My good friend,' said Socrates, 'how can I fail to be lost for words, or anyone else, who has to follow such a beautiful and varied speech? The rest was not quite so amazing; but who could fail to be struck by the beauty of language and phrasing at the end? I saw that I couldn't even get close to this degree of beauty in my speech, and was so ashamed I nearly ran away (and would have done if I'd had anywhere to go). The speech reminded me of Gorgias, and so I had just the same experience that Homer describes. I was afraid that Agathon would end his speech by directing the Gorgon-like head of the formidable orator Gorgias at my speech and turn me into speechless stone. Then I realized I'd made a fool of myself in agreeing to take my turn with you in eulogizing Love and in claiming expertise in the ways of love; in fact I knew nothing about what was involved in eulogizing something. I was so naïve that I thought you should tell the truth about the subject of the eulogy; I thought this should be the basis from which to select the finest features and present them in a way that showed the subject at its best. I took pride in thinking that I would give a good speech because I knew the truth about how to give a eulogy of a subject.

'But in fact, it seems, that isn't the right way of praising something. Instead, you should claim that your subject has the greatest and finest possible qualities, whether it really does or not; and if what you say isn't true, it doesn't matter very much. What was proposed, it seems, was that each of us should give the appearance of praising Love, not that we should actually do so. That must be why the rest of you find anything that can be said and ascribe it to Love, saying that he is like this and responsible for that, to make him look as fine and good as possible. You're obviously doing this for the ignorant (not, of course, for those who understand the subject); and your eulogies have certainly been beautiful and impressive.

'But I didn't know the right way of giving a eulogy,

and it was out of ignorance that I agreed to give one in my turn. But "it was the tongue" that promised, "not the heart"; so let's forget about it. I'm not giving another eulogy of that kind – I couldn't do it. However, I am prepared to tell the truth, if you'd like that, though in my own way, not competing with your speeches, which would make me look ridiculous. So let me know, Phaedrus, whether there's any need for a speech like that, one which tells the truth about Love, but which uses whatever words and phrases happen to occur to me as I go along.'

Phaedrus and the others told him to give his speech in whatever style he thought best.

'Phaedrus,' Socrates said, 'would you also allow me to ask Agathon a few little questions, so that I can make my speech on the basis of agreement with him?'

'I give my consent,' Phaedrus said; 'ask away.'

After that, Aristodemus said, Socrates made this start to his speech.

'My dear Agathon, I thought you made a good start to your speech, when you said that we should bring out Love's character before turning to the effects he produces. I think that's an admirable way to start. Well then, now that you've given a fine and magnificent exposition of the nature of Love in other respects, tell me this too. Is it Love's nature to be love *of* something or nothing? I'm not asking whether Love is the child *of* a particular mother or father; it would be absurd of me to ask whether Love is love *of* a mother or father in this sense. But suppose I'd asked the question, whether a father is father *of* someone or not. If you'd wanted to give the right answer, you'd surely have said that a father is father *of* a son or daughter, wouldn't you?'

'Certainly,' said Agathon.

'The same goes for a mother?'

He agreed to this too.

'Well then,' said Socrates, 'answer a little further, and you'll have a better idea of what I've got in mind. Suppose I asked this: is a brother, in so far as he is a brother, brother *of* someone or not?'

He said that he was.

'That is, a brother *of* a brother or sister?'

He agreed.

'Now try to tell me about love', he said. 'Is Love love *of* nothing or something?'

'Of something, undoubtedly!'

'For the moment,' said Socrates, 'keep to yourself and bear in mind what love is *of*. But tell me this much: does Love desire what it is love of or not?'

'Yes,' he said.

'When he desires and loves, does he have in his possession what he desires and loves or not?'

'He doesn't – at least probably not,' he said.

'Think about it,' Socrates said. 'Surely it's not just probable but necessary that desire is directed at something you need and that if you don't need something you don't desire it? I feel amazingly certain that it is necessary; what do you think?'

'I think so too,' said Agathon.

'That's right. Now would anyone who was tall want to be tall or anyone who was strong want to be strong?'

'That's impossible, according to what we've agreed already.'

'Yes, because no one is in need of qualities he already has.'

'That's true.'

'Suppose that someone who was strong wanted to be strong,' said Socrates, 'and someone who was fast wanted to be fast, and someone who was healthy wanted to be healthy. You might think that in these and all such cases people who are like that and who have those qualities also desire what they already have. I make this point to stop us getting the wrong idea. If you think about it, Agathon, these people must *necessarily* have each of the qualities they have at any one time, whether they want to or not; and so this can't be what they desire. So if someone says, "I'm healthy and want to be healthy", or "I'm rich and want to be rich", or "I desire the things that I've got", we should say to him, "My friend, you already have wealth or health or strength. What you want is to have them in the future, since at the present you have them whether you want them or not. When you say that you desire what you've already got, ask yourself whether you mean that you want what you've got now to go on being there in the future." He'd have to agree to that, wouldn't he?'

Agathon said that he would.

Socrates said, 'What someone is doing in these cases is loving something that isn't available to him and which he doesn't have, namely the continued presence in the future of the things he has now.'

'Certainly,' he said.

'So this and every other case of desire is desire for what isn't available and actually there. Desire and love are directed at what you don't have, what isn't there, and what you need.'

'Certainly,' he said.

'Come on then,' said Socrates; 'let's sum up what we've agreed. First, that Love is *of* something; second, that it is of something that he currently needs.'

'Yes,' he said.

'Now, bearing this in mind, recall what you said in your speech about what Love is *of.* If you like, I'll remind you. I think you said something like this, that the affairs of the gods were organized through love of beautiful things, since it's impossible to love ugly things. Isn't this more or less what you said?'

'Yes, I did,' Agathon said.

'What you say is plausible, my friend,' Socrates said. 'If this is right, then mustn't Love be love of beauty and not of ugliness?'

He agreed.

'Didn't we agree that he loves what he needs and doesn't have?'

'Yes,' he said.

'It follows that Love needs beauty and doesn't have it?'

'That must be the case,' he said.

'Well, would you say that something that needs beauty and is wholly without beauty is beautiful?'

'No.'

'If this is so, do you still suppose that Love is beautiful?'

Agathon said, 'It looks, Socrates, as though I didn't know what I was talking about then.'

'Ah well, it was still a beautiful speech, Agathon,' he said. 'But answer just one more small question: do you think that things that are good are also beautiful?'

'I think so.'

'Then if Love is in need of beautiful things, and good things are beautiful, he would be in need of good things?'

'I can't argue against you, Socrates,' he said. 'Let's accept that things are as you say.'

'It's the truth you can't argue against, my dear friend Agathon,' Socrates said. 'It's not at all difficult to argue against Socrates.

'Now I'll let you go. I'll try to restate for you the account of Love that I once heard from a woman from Mantinea called Diotima. She was wise about this and many other things. On one occasion, she enabled the Athenians to delay the plague for ten years by telling them what sacrifices to make. She is also the one who taught me the ways of Love. I'll report what she said, using as a basis the conclusions I reached with Agathon, but doing it on my own, as far as I can.

'As you stated, Agathon, one should first describe who Love is and what his character is and then describe his effects. I think the easiest thing is to report the content of a discussion I once had with Diotima, in which she put questions to me. I had said to her virtually the same things that Agathon said to me just now: that Love was a great god, and that he was himself beautiful. She used against me the same arguments that I used against him, proving that, according to my reasoning, Love was neither beautiful nor good.

'I said, "What do you mean, Diotima? Is Love ugly and bad then?"

'She said, "What blasphemy! Do you think that anything which isn't beautiful must necessarily be ugly?"

' "I certainly do."

' "And must anything that isn't wise be ignorant? Haven't you realized that there's something between wisdom and ignorance?"

' "What is it?"

' "It's having right opinions without being able to give reasons for having them. Don't you realize that this isn't knowing, because you don't have knowledge unless you can give reasons; but it isn't ignorance either, because ignorance has no contact with the truth? Right opinion, of course, has this kind of status, falling between understanding and ignorance."

' "You're right," I said.

' "Then don't think that what isn't beautiful must be ugly, and that what isn't good must be bad. In the same way, when you yourself agree that Love is neither good nor beautiful, don't suppose that he must therefore be ugly and bad, but something in between these two."

' "But", I said, "it's agreed by everyone that Love is a great god."

' "Do you mean everyone who doesn't know," she asked, "or do you also include those who do?"

' "Absolutely everyone."

'She laughed and said, "But Socrates, how could

people agree that Love is a great god if they deny he's a god at all?"

' "Who are these people?" I said.

' "You're one," she said, "and I'm another."

'At this I demanded, "How can you say this?"

' "Easily," she said. "Tell me, do you think that all gods are happy and beautiful? Or would you dare to suggest that any of the gods is not beautiful and happy?"

' "By Zeus, I wouldn't," I said.

' "And you call happy those who are in possession of good and beautiful things?"

' "Certainly."

' "But you've agreed that it's because Love is in need of good and beautiful things that he desires those very things that he needs."

' "Yes, I've agreed to that."

' "So how could he be a god if he is not in possession of beautiful and good things?"

' "That's impossible, as it seems."

' "Do you see, then," she said, "that you don't believe Love is a god?"

' "But what could Love be?" I said. "A mortal?"

' "Far from it."

' "What then?"

' "Like those examples discussed earlier," she said, "he's between mortal and immortal."

' "What does that make him, Diotima?"

' "He is a great spirit, Socrates. Everything classed as a spirit falls between god and human."

' "What function do they have?" I asked.

' "They interpret and carry messages from humans to gods and from gods to humans. They convey prayers and sacrifices from humans, and commands and gifts in return for sacrifices from gods. Being intermediate between the other two, they fill the gap between them, and enable the universe to form an interconnected whole. They serve as the medium for all divination, for priestly expertise in sacrifice, ritual and spells, and for all prophecy and sorcery. Gods do not make direct contact with humans; they communicate and converse with humans (whether awake or asleep) entirely through the medium of spirits. Someone whose wisdom lies in these areas is a man of the spirit, while wisdom in other areas of expertise and craftmanship makes one merely a mechanic. There are many spirits, of very different types, and one of them is Love."

' "Who are his father and mother?" I asked.

' "That's rather a long story," she replied, "but I'll tell you anyway. Following the birth of Aphrodite, the other gods were having a feast, including Resource, the son of Invention. When they'd had dinner, Poverty came to beg, as people do at feasts, and so she was by the gate. Resource was drunk with nectar (this was before wine was discovered), went into the garden of Zeus, and fell into drunken sleep. Poverty formed the plan of relieving her lack of resources by having a child by Resource; she slept with him and became pregnant with Love. So the reason Love became a follower and attendant of Aphrodite is because he was conceived on the day of her birth; also he is naturally a lover of beauty and Aphrodite is beautiful.

' "Because he is the son of Resource and Poverty, Love's situation is like this. First of all, he's always poor; far from being sensitive and beautiful, as is commonly supposed, he's tough, with hardened skin, without shoes or home. He always sleeps rough, on the ground, with no bed, lying in doorways and by roads in the open air; sharing his mother's nature, he always lives in a state of need. On the other hand, taking after his father, he schemes to get hold of beautiful and good things. He's brave, impetutous and intense; a formidable hunter, always weaving tricks; he desires knowledge and is re-sourceful in getting it; a lifelong lover of wisdom; clever at using magic, drugs and sophistry.

' "By nature he is neither immortal nor mortal. Some-times on a single day he shoots into life, when he's successful, and then dies, and then (taking after his father) comes back to life again. The resources he obtains keep on draining away, so that Love is neither wholly without resources nor rich. He is also in between wisdom and ignorance. The position is this. None of the gods loves wisdom or has the desire to become wise – because they already are; nor does anyone else who is already wise love wisdom. Nor do the ignorant love wisdom or have the desire to become wise. The problem with the ignor-ant person is precisely that, despite not being good or intelligent, he regards himself as satisfactory. If someone doesn't think he's in need of something, he can't desire what he doesn't think he needs."

' "Who are the lovers of wisdom, Diotima," I asked, "if they are neither the wise nor the ignorant?"

' "Even a child", she said, "would realize by now that

it is those who fall between these two, and that Love is one of them. Wisdom is one of the most beautiful things, and Love is love of beauty. So Love must necessarily be a lover of wisdom; and as a lover of wisdom he falls between wisdom and ignorance. Again the reason for this is his origin: his father is wise and resourceful while his mother has neither quality. So this is the nature of the spirit of Love, my dear Socrates. But it's not at all surprising that you took the view of Love you did. To judge from what you said, I think you saw Love as the object of love instead of the lover: that's why you imagined that Love is totally beautiful. But in fact beauty, elegance, perfection and blessedness are characteristic of the object that deserves to be loved, while the lover has a quite different character, which I have described."

' "Well, Diotima," I said, "I'm sure you're right about this. But if Love is like that, what use is he to human beings?"

' "That's the next thing, Socrates," she said; "I'll try to teach you. So far we've dealt with Love's nature and birth; also, according to you, love is *of* beautiful things. But then, supposing someone asked us, '*Why* is Love of beautiful things?', or, to put it more clearly, 'The lover of beautiful things has a desire – what is it that he desires?' "

' "That they become his own," I said.

' "But this answer raises another question," she said. "What will he get when beautiful things become his own?"

'I said that I didn't have a ready answer to that question.

' "But suppose", she said, "someone changed the question, using the word 'good' instead of 'beautiful', and asked: 'Now then, Socrates, the lover of good things has a desire – what is it that he desires?' "

' "That they become his own," I said.

' "And what will he get when good things become his own?"

' "That's easier for me to answer," I said; "he'll be happy."

' "So it's the ownership of good things that makes happy people happy; and you don't need to ask the further question, 'Why does someone want to be happy?' This answer seems to mark the end of the enquiry."

' "That's true," I said.

' "Do you think that this wish and this form of love are common to all human beings, and that everyone wants good things to be his own forever, or what is your view?"

' "Just that," I said; "it's common to everyone."

' "In that case, Socrates," she said, "why don't we say that everyone is a lover, if everyone always loves the same things; why do we call some people lovers and not others?"

' "That's something I've wondered about too," I said.

' "It's nothing to wonder about," she said. "What we're doing is picking out one kind of love and applying to it the name ('love') that belongs to the whole class, while we use different names for other kinds of love."

' "Can you give me another example?" I asked.

' "Yes, this one. You know that composition forms a general class. When anything comes into being which

did not exist before, the cause of this is always composition. So the products of all the crafts are compositions
and the craftsmen who make them are all composers?"

'"That's right," I said.

'"But you know that they aren't called composers
but have different names. Out of the whole class of
composition we pick out one part, the one related to
music and verse, and call that by the name of the class
as a whole. It's only this that's called composition and
those who have this subdivision of the skill are called
composers."

'"That's right," I said.

'"The same goes for love. In essence, every type of
desire for good things or happiness is what constitutes,
in all cases, 'powerful and treacherous love'. But this can
be approached by many routes, and those who do so by
other means, such as making money or athletics or
philosophy, aren't described as 'loving' or 'lovers'. It's
only those whose enthusiasm is directed at one specific
type who are described by the terminology that belongs
to the whole class, that of love, loving and lovers."

'"I suppose that's right," I said.

'"The idea has been put forward", she said, "that
lovers are people who are looking for their own other
halves. But my view is that love is directed neither at
their half nor their whole unless, my friend, that turns
out to be good. After all, people are even prepared to
have their own feet or hands amputated if they think
that those parts of themselves are diseased. I don't think
that each of us is attached to his own characteristics,
unless you're going to describe the good as 'his own'

and as 'what belongs to him', and the bad as 'what does not belong to him'. The point is that the only object of people's love is the good – don't you agree?"

' "By Zeus, I do!" I said.

' "Well then," she said, "can we quite simply say that people love the good?"

' "Yes," I said.

' "But shouldn't we add," she said, "that the object of their love is that they should have the good?"

' "Yes, we should add that."

' "Not only that," she said, "but that they should have the good forever."

' "We must add that too."

' "To sum up then," she said, "love is the desire to have the good forever."

' "What you say is absolutely right," I said.

' "Given that love always has this overall goal," she said, "we should also ask this. In what way and in what type of action must people pursue this goal, if the enthusiasm and intensity they show in this pursuit is to be called love? What function does love really have: can you tell me?"

' "If I could, Diotima," I said, "I wouldn't be so amazed at your wisdom, and wouldn't keep coming to you as your student to learn these very things."

' "Then I shall tell you," she said. "Love's function is giving birth in beauty both in body and in mind."

' "One would need to be a prophet to interpret what you're saying," I said. "I don't understand it."

' "Well," she said, "I'll explain it more clearly. All human beings are pregnant in body and in mind, and

when we reach a degree of adulthood we naturally desire
to give birth. We cannot give birth in what is ugly, only
in what is beautiful. Yes, sexual intercourse between
men and women is a kind of birth. There is something
divine in this process; this is how mortal creatures
achieve immortality, in pregnancy and giving birth. This
cannot occur in a condition of disharmony. The ugly is
out of harmony with everything divine, while the beautiful fits in with it. So Beauty is the goddess who, as Fate
or Eileithyia, presides over childbirth. That's why, when
a pregnant creature comes close to something beautiful,
it becomes gentle and joyfully relaxed, and gives birth
and reproduces. But when it comes close to something
ugly, it frowns and contracts in pain; it turns away and
shrivels up and does not reproduce; it holds the foetus
inside and is in discomfort. That's why those who are
pregnant and already swollen get so excited about
beauty: the bearer of beauty enables them to gain release
from the pains of childbirth. You see, Socrates," she said,
"the object of love is not beauty, as you suppose."

' "What is it then?"

' "Reproduction and birth in beauty."

' "That may well be so," I said.

' "It certainly is," she said. "And why is reproduction
the object of love? Because reproduction is the closest
mortals can come to being permanently alive and immortal. If what we agreed earlier is right, that the object of
love is to have the good *always*, it follows that we must
desire immortality along with the good. It follows from
this argument that the object of love must be immortality
as well."

'Diotima taught me all this in her talks with me about the ways of love. One day she asked, "What do you think, Socrates, is the cause of this love and desire? Haven't you noticed what a terrible state animals of all kinds (footed beasts as well as winged birds) get into when they feel the desire to reproduce. They are all sick with the excitement of love, that makes them first want to have sex with each other and then to rear what they have brought into being. Even the weakest of animals are ready to fight with the strongest and die for the sake of their young; they are prepared to be racked with hunger themselves in order to provide food for their young, and to do anything else for them. Humans, you might think, do this because they understand the reason for it; but, in the case of animals, what causes this excitement of love – can you tell me?"

'I said again that I didn't know.

'She said, "Do you think you'll ever become an expert in the ways of love if you don't understand this?"

' "But that's why I come to study with you, Diotima, as I said before, because I realize I need teachers. So tell me the reason for this, and for everything else connected with the ways of love."

' "Well then," she said, "if you believe that the natural object of love is what we've often agreed, you shouldn't be surprised at this. The point made about humans applies also to animals; mortal nature does all it can to live forever and to be immortal. It can only do this by reproduction: it always leaves behind another, new generation to replace the old. This point applies even in the period in which each living creature is described as alive and as the same – for instance, someone is said to be the same person from childhood till old age. Although he is called the same person, he never has the same constituents, but is always being renewed in some respects and experiencing loss in others, for instance, his hair, skin, bone, blood and his whole body. This applies not only to the body but also to the mind: attributes, character-traits, beliefs, desires, pleasures, pains, fears – none of these ever remain the same in each of us, but some are emerging while others are being lost. Still more remarkable is the fact that our knowledge changes too, some items emerging, while others are lost, so we are not the same person as regards our knowledge; indeed, each individual item of knowledge goes through the same process. What is called studying exists because knowledge goes from us. Forgetting is the departure of knowledge, while study puts back new information in our memory to replace what is lost, and so maintains knowledge so that it seems to be the same.

' "This is the way that every mortal thing is maintained in existence, not by being completely the same, as divine things are, but because everything that grows old and goes away leaves behind another new thing of the same type. This is the way, Socrates, that mortal things have a share in immortality, physically and in all other ways; but immortal things do so in a different way. So you shouldn't be surprised if everything naturally values its own offspring. It's to achieve immortality that everything shows this enthusiasm, which is what love is."

'But in fact, when I heard her speech, I was surprised

and said, "Well, Diotima, you're very wise, but are things really as you say?"

'Like a perfect sophist, she said, "You can be sure about this. You can see the same principle at work if you look at the way people love honour. You'd be amazed at your own stupidity if you failed to see the point of what I've said, after considering how terribly they are affected by love of becoming famous 'and storing up immortal fame for eternity'. They are readier even to risk every danger for this than for their children's sake, and to spend money, suffer any kind of ordeal, and die for honour. Do you think", she said, "that Alcestis would have died for Admetus, or that Achilles would have added his death to that of Patroclus, or that your Athenian hero Codrus would have died to defend his sons' kingdom, if they had not thought that the memory of their courage (which we still hold in respect) would last forever? They certainly wouldn't," she said. "I think it is undying virtue and glorious fame of this sort that motivates everyone in all they do, and the better they are, the more true this is; it's immortality they are in love with.

'"Men who are pregnant in body," she said, "are drawn more towards women; they express their love in trying to obtain for themselves immortality and remembrance and what they take to be happiness forever by producing children. Men who are pregnant in mind – there are some," she said, "who are even more pregnant in their minds than in their bodies, and are pregnant with what it is suitable for a mind to bear and bring to birth. So what is suitable? Wisdom and other kinds of virtue: these are brought to birth by all the poets and by those craftsmen who are said to be innovative. Much the most important and finest type of wisdom", she said, "is that connected with the organization of cities and households, which is called moderation and justice. Take also the case of someone who's been pregnant in mind with these virtues from a young age. When he's still without a partner and reaches adulthood, he feels the desire to give birth and reproduce. He too, I think, goes around looking for beauty in which to reproduce; he will never do so in ugliness. Because he's pregnant, he's attracted to beautiful bodies rather than ugly ones; and if he's also lucky enough to find a mind that is beautiful, noble and naturally gifted, he is strongly drawn to this combination. With someone like this, he immediately finds he has the resources to talk about virtue and about what a good man should be like and should do, and tries to educate him.

' "It is, I think, when someone has made contact and formed a relationship with beauty of this sort that he gives birth to, and reproduces, the child with which he has long been pregnant. He thinks about the other's beauty, whether they are in each other's company or not, and together with him he shares in bringing up the child reproduced in this way. People like that have a much closer partnership with each other and a stronger bond of friendship than parents have, because the children of their partnership are more beautiful and more immortal. Everyone would prefer to have children like that rather than human ones. People look enviously at

Homer and Hesiod and other good poets, because of the kind of children they have left behind them, which provide them with immortal fame and remembrance by being immortal themselves. Or take," she said, "the children that Lycurgus left in Sparta to provide security to Sparta and, you might say, to Greece as a whole. Solon is also respected by you Athenians for the laws he fathered; and other men, in very different places, in Greece and other countries, have exhibited many fine achievements and generated virtue of every type. Many cults have been set up to honour these men as a result of children of that kind, but this has never happened as a result of human children.

'"Even you, Socrates, could perhaps be initiated in the rites of love I've described so far. But the purpose of these rites, if they are performed correctly, is to reach the final vision of the mysteries; and I'm not sure you could manage this. But I'll tell you about them," she said, "and make every effort in doing so; try to follow, as far as you can.

'"The correct way", she said, "for someone to approach this business is to begin when he's young by being drawn towards beautiful bodies. At first, if his guide leads him correctly, he should love just one body and in that relationship produce beautiful discourses. Next he should realize that the beauty of any one body is closely related to that of another, and that, if he is to pursue beauty of form, it's very foolish not to regard the beauty of all bodies as one and the same. Once he's seen this, he'll become a lover of all beautiful bodies, and will relax his intense passion for just one body, despising this passion and regarding it as petty. After this, he should regard the beauty of minds as more valuable than that of the body, so that, if someone has goodness of mind even if he has little of the bloom of beauty, he will be content with him, and will love and care for him, and give birth to the kinds of discourse that help young men to become better. As a result, he will be forced to observe the beauty in practices and laws and to see that every type of beauty is closely related to every other, so that he will regard beauty of body as something petty. After practices, the guide must lead him towards forms of knowledge, so that he sees their beauty too. Looking now at beauty in general and not just at individual instances, he will no longer be slavishly attached to the beauty of a boy, or of any particular person at all, or of a specific practice. Instead of this low and small-minded slavery, he will be turned towards the great sea of beauty and gazing on it he'll give birth, through a boundless love of knowledge, to many beautiful and magnificent discourses and ideas. At last, when he has been developed and strengthened in this way, he catches sight of one special type of knowledge, whose object is the kind of beauty I shall now describe.

'"Now try", she said, "to concentrate as hard as you can. Anyone who has been educated this far in the ways of love, viewing beautiful things in the right order and way, will now reach the goal of love's ways. He will suddenly catch sight of something amazingly beautiful in its nature; this, Socrates, is the ultimate objective of all the previous efforts. First, this beauty always *is*, and doesn't come into being or cease; it doesn't increase or diminish. Second, it's not beautiful in one respect but ugly in another, or beautiful at one time but not at another, or beautiful in relation to this but ugly in relation to that; nor beautiful here and ugly there because it is beautiful for some people but ugly for others. Nor will beauty appear to him in the form of a face or hands or any part of the body; or as a specific account or piece of knowledge; or as being anywhere in something else, for instance in a living creature or earth or heaven or anything else. It will appear as in itself and by itself, always single in form; all other beautiful things share its character, but do so in such a way that, when other things come to be or cease, it is not increased or decreased in any way nor does it undergo any change.

'"When someone goes up by these stages, through loving boys in the correct way, and begins to catch sight of that beauty, he has come close to reaching the goal. This is the right method of approaching the ways of love or being led by someone else: beginning from these beautiful things always to go up with the aim of reaching that beauty. Like someone using a staircase, he should go from one to two and from two to all beautiful bodies, and from beautiful bodies to beautiful practices, and from practices to beautiful forms of learning. From forms of learning, he should end up at that form of learning which is of nothing other than *that* beauty itself, so that he can complete the process of learning what beauty really is.

'"In that form of life, my dear Socrates," said the Mantinean stranger, "if in any, human life should be lived, gazing on beauty itself. If you ever saw that, it would seem to be on a different level from gold and clothes and beautiful boys and young men. At present you're so overwhelmed when you see these that you're ready, together with many others, to look at your boy-friends and be with them forever, if that was somehow possible, doing without food and drink and doing nothing but gazing at them and being with them. So what should we imagine it would be like", she said, "if someone could see beauty itself, absolute, pure, unmixed, not cluttered up with human flesh and colours and a great mass of mortal rubbish, but if he could catch sight of divine beauty itself, in its single form? Do you think", she said, "that would be a poor life for a human being, looking in that direction and gazing at that object with the right part of himself and sharing its company? Don't you realize," she said, "that it's only in that kind of life, when someone sees beauty with the part that can see it, that he'll be able to give birth not just to images of virtue (since it's not images he's in touch with), but to true virtue (since it's true beauty he's in touch with). It's someone who's given birth to true virtue and brought it up who has the chance of becoming loved by the gods, and immortal – if any human being can be immortal."

'Well, Phaedrus and the rest of you, this is what Diotima said, and I was convinced. Because I was convinced, I try to convince others that, to acquire this possession, you couldn't easily find a better partner for human nature than Love. That's the basis for my claiming that every man should hold Love in respect, and I myself respect the ways of love and practise them with exceptional care. That's why I urge others to do the same, and on this and every other occasion I do all I can to praise the power and courage of Love. So this is my speech, Phaedrus. If you like, you can think of it as a eulogy of Love or if you prefer, you can give it whatever name you like to give it.'

After Socrates' speech, Aristodemus said, while the others congratulated him, Aristophanes was trying to make a point, because Socrates had referred to his speech at some stage. Suddenly, there was a loud noise of knocking at the front door, which sounded like revellers, and they heard the voice of a flute-girl.

'Slaves, go and see who it is,' Agathon said. 'If it's any of my friends, invite them in; if not, tell them the symposium's over and we're just now going to bed.'

Not long after, they heard the voice of Alcibiades in the courtyard; he was very drunk and was shouting loudly, asking where Agathon was and demanding to be brought to him. He was brought in, supported by the flute-girl and some of the other people in his group. He stood by the door, wearing a thick garland of ivy and violets, with masses of ribbons trailing over his head, and said:

'Good evening, gentlemen. Will you let someone who's drunk – very drunk – join your symposium? Or should we just put a garland on Agathon, which is why we've come, and go away? I couldn't come to your celebration yesterday,' he said. 'But I've come now with the ribbons on my head, so that I can transfer them directly from my head to that of the man who is – I'd like to announce – the wisest and most beautiful. I suppose you'll laugh at me because I'm drunk. But even

Plato

if you laugh at me, I know quite well I'm telling the truth. But tell me right away whether I can come in on these terms or not. Can I join you for a drink, or not?'

Everyone shouted out, telling him to come in and take a place on a couch, and Agathon invited him too. So he came in, supported by his friends. He was untying the ribbons to tie them on Agathon, and they fell over his eyes. So he didn't notice Socrates, but sat down next to Agathon, between him and Socrates, who moved over when he saw him. When he'd sat down, he embraced Agathon and tied the garland round his head.

Agathon said, 'Take off his sandals, slaves, so that he can lie down and be the third on this couch.'

'Fine,' said Alcibiades; 'but who's this third person drinking with us?' As he said this, he turned round and saw Socrates. When he saw him, he jumped up and said, 'Oh Heracles, what's going on here? Is this Socrates? You've been lying here in wait for me again, so that you can play your usual trick of turning up suddenly wherever I least expect you. Why have you come here? And why did you choose this couch? I see you didn't pick Aristophanes or anyone else who's prepared to make a fool of himself, but you made sure you'd be lying beside the most attractive man in the room.'

Socrates said, 'Agathon, please protect me. What a nuisance my love for this man has become! Ever since I started loving him, I haven't been able to look at or talk to a single attractive man without his getting so jealous and resentful that he goes crazy and shouts at me and almost beats me up. So make sure that he doesn't do anything to me now and make peace between us; or if

64

he starts to get violent, protect me from him. I'm quite terrified by his mad attachment to his lovers.'

'There can be no peace between me and you,' Alcibiades said. 'I'll get my own back on you for this another time. But for now, Agathon,' he said, 'give me back some of those ribbons, so that I can tie them on this amazing head of his. Otherwise, he'll criticize me for tying them on your head, not his, even though he *always* beats off all comers in verbal contest – and you've just done it once, two days ago.'

As he spoke, he took some of the ribbons, and tied them on Socrates, and lay down again. When he settled down, he said, 'Well, gentlemen, you look sober to me. This can't be allowed; you have to drink. This was what we agreed. For our master of ceremonies, to take charge of the drinking, until you're drunk enough, I elect – myself! Have a big goblet brought in, Agathon, if you've got one. Or rather, there's no need; bring me, boy, that wine-cooler,' he said, seeing one that held more than four pints. He had this filled up, and drank it down himself, and then he told the slave to fill it up for Socrates. As he did so, he said, 'Not that my trick will have any effect on Socrates, gentlemen. However much you tell him to drink, he drinks without ever getting more drunk.'

The slave filled it for Socrates and, while he was drinking it, Eryximachus said, 'What sort of behaviour is this, Alcibiades? Aren't we going to have any conversation or songs as we pass round the cup, but do nothing but drink as though we were thirsty?'

Alcibiades said, 'Hello, Eryximachus, best of sons of the best – and most temperate – of fathers.'

'Hello to you too,' Eryximachus said; 'but what should we do?'

'Whatever you tell us. We should obey you, because "a doctor is equal in worth to many other men"; so tell us to do whatever you want.'

'Listen to me then,' Eryximachus said. 'Before you arrived, we'd decided to take turns, going round from left to right, making the finest speech each of us could, in praise of Love. All the rest of us have given our speeches. You haven't taken your turn at speaking, though you've done well at drinking, so it's right for you to make a speech. Once you've spoken, you can order Socrates to do whatever you want, and he can do the same to the person on his right and so on.'

'That's a good idea, Eryximachus,' Alcibiades said. 'But I don't think it's fair to make someone who's drunk compete against speeches made by people when they were sober. Also, my dear friend, I hope you don't believe any of what Socrates just said. Don't you realize that the truth is quite the opposite of what he said? If I praise anyone else, whether god or human, while he's around, it's he who'll beat *me* up.'

'What blasphemy!' Socrates said.

'By Poseidon!' Alcibiades said, 'don't contradict me on this point. I'm never going to praise anyone else while you're around.'

'Well then, do just that, if you want,' Eryximachus said. 'Give a eulogy of Socrates.'

'What do you mean?' said Alcibiades. 'Do you think I should, Eryximachus? Should I attack him and punish him in front of you all?'

'Hang on,' said Socrates. 'What are you planning – to give a eulogy that makes fun of me, or what?'

'I'll tell the truth – will you let me do that?'

'But of course I'll let you tell the truth; indeed, I order you to.'

'Here I go then,' Alcibiades said. 'But this is what you can do. If I say anything that isn't true, interrupt, if you like, and point out that what I'm saying is false. I don't want to say anything that's false. But if I don't remember things in the right order, don't be surprised. It isn't easy for someone in my condition to list all the aspects of your peculiarity in a fluent and orderly sequence.

'The way I'll try to praise Socrates, gentlemen, is through images. Perhaps he'll think this is to make fun of him; but the image will be designed to bring out the truth not to make fun. My claim is that he's just like those statues of Silenus you see sitting in sculptors' shops. The figures are produced holding shepherd's pipes or flutes; when they're opened up, you find they've got statues of the gods inside. I also claim he's like Marsyas the satyr. Not even you, Socrates, could deny that you resemble these in appearance; but you're going to hear next how you're like them in other ways too.

'You're insulting and abusive, aren't you? If you don't admit this, I'll provide witnesses. And aren't you a flute-player? In fact, you're a much more amazing one than Marsyas. He used instruments to bewitch people with the power of his mouth, and so does anyone who plays his flute-music today. (I'm counting the tunes of Olympus as really Marsyas', because Marsyas was Olympus' teacher.) Whether these tunes are played by an expert player or a poor flute-girl, they're the only ones which, because of their divine origin, can cast a spell over people and so show which ones are ready for the gods and initiation into the mysteries. The only difference between you and Marsyas is that you produce this same effect without the use of instruments, by words alone. Whenever we hear someone else making speeches, even if he's a very good orator, this has virtually no impact on any of us. But whenever anyone hears you speak or hears your words reported by someone else (even if he's a very poor speaker), whoever we are – woman, man or boy – we're overwhelmed and spellbound.

'If it weren't for the fact that you'd think I was completely drunk, gentlemen, I'd take an oath on the truth of what I'm saying about the effect his words have had on me – an effect they still have now. Whenever I listen to him, my frenzy is greater than that of the Corybantes. My heart pounds and tears flood out when he speaks, and I see that many other people are affected in the same way. I've heard Pericles and other good orators, and I thought they spoke well. But they haven't produced this kind of effect on me; they haven't disturbed my whole personality and made me dissatisfied with the slavish quality of my life. But this Marsyas here has often had this effect on me, and made me think that the life I'm leading isn't worth living. You can't say this isn't true, Socrates. Even now I'm well aware that if I allowed myself to listen to him I couldn't resist but would have the same experience again. He makes me admit that, in spite of my great defects, I neglect myself and instead get involved in Athenian politics. So I force myself to block my ears and go away, like someone escaping from the Sirens, to prevent myself sitting there beside him till I grow old.

'He's the only person in whose company I've had an experience you might think me incapable of – feeling shame with someone; I only feel shame in his company. I'm well aware that I can't argue against him and that I should do what he tells me; but when I leave him, I'm carried away by the people's admiration. So I act like a runaway slave and escape from him; and whenever I see him, I'm ashamed because of what he's made me agree to. Often I've felt I'd be glad to see him removed from the human race; but if this did happen, I know well I'd be much more upset. I just don't know how to deal with this person.

'This is the effect this satyr has had on me and many other people with his flute-playing. Listen to other ways that he's like these creatures I'm comparing him with and what amazing power he has. You should realize that none of you really knows him. But I'll show what he's like, now that I've made a start. You see that Socrates is erotically attracted to beautiful boys, and is always hanging around them in a state of excitement. Also he's completely ignorant and knows nothing. In giving this impression, isn't he like Silenus? Very much so. This behaviour is just his outer covering, like that of the statues of Silenus. But if you could open him up and look inside, you can't imagine, my fellow-drinkers, how full of moderation he is! You should know that he doesn't care at all if someone is beautiful – he regards this with unbelievable contempt – or is rich or has any of the other advantages prized by ordinary people. He regards all these possessions as worthless and regards us as worth nothing too (believe me!). He spends his whole life pretending and playing with people.

'I don't know if any of you have seen the statues inside Socrates when he's serious and is opened up. But I saw them once, and they seemed to me so divine, golden, so utterly beautiful and amazing, that – to put it briefly – I had to do whatever Socrates told me to. I thought he was seriously interested in my looks and that this was a godsend and an amazing piece of good luck, because, if I gratified him, I'd be able to hear everything he knew. You see, I was incredibly proud of my good looks. Before this, I had never been alone with him without an attendant; but once I'd got this idea I sent the attendant away and was with him on my own. Yes, I must tell you the whole truth; so pay careful attention, and, if I say anything that's not right, Socrates, you must contradict me.

'Well, there we were, gentlemen, the two of us on our own. I thought he would immediately have the kind of conversation with me that lovers have with their boyfriends when they're on their own, and I was pleased by that thought. But nothing like that happened at all. He had his usual kind of conversation with me and went away after spending the day with me. After that I invited him to come to the gymnasium with me and we exercised together; I thought I would get somewhere that way. So we exercised together and wrestled on many occasions with no one around – and what can I tell you? I got nowhere.

'Since I was getting nowhere by these means, I decided to make a direct assault on the man, and not to give up now that I'd made a start. I felt I had to know how things stood. I invited him to dinner, just as though I were the lover and he the boy I had designs on. He wasn't quick to accept my invitation, but eventually agreed to come. The first time he came, he wanted to go after dinner, and on that occasion I was ashamed and let him go. But I continued my plan another time, and when we'd had dinner I kept the conversation going far into the night. Then, when he wanted to go, I made the excuse that it was too late to go, and made him stay. So he settled down to sleep on the couch next to mine, where he'd had dinner, and there was no one else sleeping in the room but us.

'Up to this point, it would have been all right for anyone to hear what I've said. But from now on there are things you wouldn't have heard me say except that, as the saying goes, "there's truth in wine when the slaves have left", and when they haven't! Also, I think it would be wrong of me to let Socrates' proud action pass into oblivion now that I've embarked on his eulogy. Besides, my experience is that of someone bitten by a snake. They say that someone who's had this experience is only prepared to say what it's like to those who've been bitten themselves, because they're the only ones who'll understand and make allowances if the pain drives you to do and say shocking things. I've been bitten by something more painful still, and in the place where a bite is most painful – the heart or mind, or whatever you should call it. I've been struck and bitten by the words of philosophy, which cling on more fiercely than a snake when they take hold of a young and talented mind, and make someone do and say all sorts of things. Also I can see here people like Phaedrus, Agathon, Eryximachus, Pausanias, Aristodemus and Aristophanes – I don't need to mention Socrates himself – and the rest of you. You've all shared the madness and Bacchic frenzy of philosophy, and so you will all hear what I have to say. You will all make allowances for what I did then and what I'm saying now. But you, house-slaves, and any other crude uninitiates, put big doors on your ears!

'So, gentlemen, when the lamp was out and the slaves had left the room, I decided I shouldn't beat about the bush but tell him openly what I had in mind. I gave him a push and said, "Socrates, are you asleep?"

'"Not at all," he said.

'"Do you know what I've been thinking?"

'"What exactly?" he said.

'"I think", I said, "you're the only lover I've ever had who's good enough for me, but you seem to be too shy to talk about it to me. I'll tell you how I feel about this. I think I'd be very foolish not to gratify you in this or in anything else you need from my property or my friends. Nothing is more important to me than becoming as good a person as possible, and I don't think anyone can help me more effectively than you can in reaching this aim. I'd be far more ashamed of what sensible people would think if I failed to gratify someone like you than of what ordinary, foolish people would think if I did."

'He listened to what I said, and then he said this, in a highly ironic manner and one that was entirely typical of him: "My dear Alcibiades, it looks as though you're really no fool, if what you say about me is true and I somehow do have the capacity to make you a better person. You must be seeing in me a beauty beyond comparison and one that's far superior to your own good looks. If you've seen this and are trying to strike a deal with me in which we exchange one type of beauty for another, you're planning to make a good profit from me. You're trying to get true beauty in return for its appearance, and so to make an exchange that is really 'gold for bronze'. But look more closely, my good friend, and make sure you're not making a mistake in thinking I'm of value to you. The mind's sight begins to see sharply when eyesight declines, and you're a long way from that point."

'When I heard this, I said, "As far as I'm concerned, this is the position, and my plans are exactly as I've said. It's now up to you to consider what you think is best for you and for me."

'"Well," he said, "you're right about that at least. In the future we'll consider and do whatever seems best to us, both in this and in other things too."

'When he made this reply to what I'd said, now that I'd fired my shots, I thought he'd been wounded. I got up from my couch, and without letting him say anything more I wrapped him in my thick outdoor cloak (it was winter then) and lay down under his short cloak. Then I threw my arms round this really god-like and amazing man, and lay there with him all night long. And you can't say this is a lie, Socrates. After I'd done all this, he completely triumphed over my good looks – and despised, scorned and insulted them – although I placed a very high value on these looks, gentlemen of the jury. I'm calling you that because you've become the jury in the case of Socrates' arrogance! I swear to you by the gods, and by the goddesses, that when I got up next morning I had no more *slept with* Socrates than if I'd been sleeping with my father or elder brother.

'After that, what state of mind do you think I was in? Although I felt I'd been humiliated, I admired his character, his self-control and courage. Here was someone with a degree of understanding and tough-mindedness I'd never expected to find. So, although I couldn't be angry with him or do without his company, I didn't know how to win him over. I knew well that he was more completely invulnerable to the power of money than Ajax was to weapons; and what I'd seen as the only means of catching him had proved a failure. I was baffled; and I went around more completely enslaved to this person than anyone else has ever been to anyone.

'It was after these events had occurred that we served together in the Athenian campaign against Potidaea and shared the same mess there. The first thing to note is that he put up with the rigours of warfare better than me – better than everyone else, in fact. When we were cut off, and forced to do without food, as sometimes happens on campaign, no one came near him in putting up with this. But on the other hand when we had a feast, he was best able to enjoy it. For instance, though reluctant to drink, when he was forced to, he beat us all at it. The most amazing thing of all is that no one has ever seen Socrates drunk. I think you'll see proof of this shortly.

'Also when it came to putting up with winter (the winters there are terrible), his endurance was remarkable. On one occasion there was such a bitter frost that no one went outside, or if they did, they wrapped themselves up with clothes in the most amazing way and tied on extra pieces of felt or sheepskin over their boots. But Socrates went out in this weather wearing the same outdoor cloak he'd usually worn before, and he made better progress over the ice in his bare feet than the rest of us did in boots. The soldiers regarded him with suspicion, thinking that he was looking down on them.

'So much for that incident; but "what the stout-hearted man did and endured next" on campaign there is well worth hearing. One morning he started thinking about a problem and stood there considering it, and when he didn't make progress with it he didn't give up but kept standing there examining it. When it got to midday, people noticed him and said to each other in amazement that Socrates had been standing there thinking about something since dawn. In the end, when it was evening, some of the Ionians, after they'd had dinner, brought their bedding outside (it was summer then), partly to sleep in the cool, and partly to keep an eye on Socrates to see if he would go on standing there through the night too. He stood there till it was dawn and the sun came up; then he greeted the sun with a prayer and went away.

'If you'd like to know what he was like in battle – here

it's right for me to repay a debt to him. During the battle after which the generals awarded me the prize for bravery, it was Socrates, no one else, who rescued me. He wasn't prepared to leave me when I was wounded and so he saved my life as well as my armour and weapons. I actually told the generals to award the prize for bravery on that occasion to you, Socrates. This is a point on which you can't criticize me or say that I'm lying. But when the generals wanted to award the prize to me, influenced by my social status, you yourself were keener than the generals that I should receive it.

'Here's another thing, gentlemen. Socrates was a sight worth seeing when the army made a disorderly retreat from Delium. It turned out that I was serving in the cavalry there while he was a hoplite. People had scattered by then in all directions, and he was retreating together with Laches. As it happened, I was near by, and when I saw them I encouraged them at once, and told them I wouldn't leave them behind. I was better able to watch Socrates there than at Potidaea (because I was on horse-back I was less worried about my safety), and the first thing that struck me was how much more self-possessed he was than Laches. Next, I noticed that he was walking along there, just as he does here in Athens – to use your phrase, Aristophanes – "swaggering and looking from side to side". He was calmly looking out both for friends and enemies, and it was obvious to everyone even from a long distance that if anyone tackled this man, he would put up a tough resistance. That was how he and his companion got safely away. Generally, people don't tackle those who show this kind of attitude in combat;

they prefer to chase those who are in headlong flight.

'There are many other remarkable things which you could say in praise of Socrates. Some of these distinctive features could perhaps also be attributed to other people too. But what is most amazing about him is that he is like no other human being, either of the past or the present. If you wanted to say what Achilles was like, you could compare him with Brasidas or others, and in Pericles' case you could compare him with Nestor or Antenor (and there are other possibilities), and you could draw other comparisons in the same way. But this person is so peculiar, and so is the way he talks, that however hard you look you'll never find anyone close to him either from the present or the past. The best you can do is what I did, in fact, when I compared him, and his way of talking, not with human beings but with Sileni and satyrs.

'This is something I forgot to say at the beginning: his discussions are also very like those Sileni that you open up. If you're prepared to listen to Socrates' discussions, they seem absolutely ridiculous at first. This is because of the words and phrases he uses, which are like the rough skin of an insulting satyr. He talks about pack-asses, blacksmiths, shoemakers and tanners, and seems to be always using the same words to make the same points; and so anyone unused to him or unintelligent would find his arguments ridiculous. But if you can open them up and see inside, you'll find they're the only ones that make any sense. You'll also find they're the most divine and contain the most images of virtue. They range over most – or rather all – of the subjects that you must examine if you're going to become a good person.

'This is what I have to say, gentlemen, in praise of Socrates. I've also mixed in some blame as well, and told you how he insulted me. I'm not the only one he's done this to; there's also Charmides the son of Glaucon, Euthydemus the son of Diocles and many others. He deceives them into thinking he's their lover and then turns out to be the loved one instead of the lover. I'm warning you, Agathon, not to be deceived by him, but to learn from what we've suffered and be cautious, and don't, as the proverb puts it, be the fool who only learns by his own suffering.'

This speech of Alcibiades created much amusement at his frankness, because he seemed to be still in love with Socrates. Socrates said, 'I think you're sober after all, Alcibiades. Otherwise you wouldn't have been able to conceal the motive of your entire speech by ingeniously disguising it in this way. You slipped it in at the end as though it was an afterthought – as though the point of the whole speech hadn't been to make trouble between myself and Agathon. You did this because you think that I should love you and no one else, and that Agathon should be loved by you and no one else. But you haven't got away with it; we've seen the purpose of this satyr-play – and Silenus-play – of yours. But, my dear Agathon, don't let him succeed in this; make sure that no one comes between me and you.'

Then Agathon said, 'You know, Socrates, I think you must be right. It's significant that he lay down in the middle, between me and you, to keep us apart. But he

won't succeed in doing this. I'll come round and lie down
beside you.'

'Please do,' said Socrates; 'come here and lie down on
the other side.'

'Oh Zeus!' said Alcibiades, 'what I suffer from this
person! He thinks he always has to get the better of me.
But if nothing else – you amazing man – let Agathon lie
down between us.'

'But that's impossible,' Socrates said. 'You've praised
me, and now it's my turn to praise the one on my right.
If Agathon lies down between us, won't he too have to
praise me, instead of being praised by me? For goodness'
sake, don't stop the young man from being praised by
me; I feel a strong desire to give his eulogy.'

'Hurrah!' said Agathon. 'Alcibiades, there's no way
I'm going to stay here now. I simply must change positions and be praised by Socrates.'

'Here we go again,' said Alcibiades; 'it's always the
same. When Socrates is around, no one else can get a
look-in with the attractive men. Now, too, see how
resourcefully he's found a plausible reason why this one
should lie down beside him.'

So Agathon got up to go and lie down beside Socrates.
Suddenly, a large group of revellers came to the front
door. They found it open because someone was just
going out; so they marched straight in to join them,
and settled themselves down on the couches. There
was noise everywhere, and all order was abandoned;
everyone was forced to drink vast amounts of wine.
Aristodemus said that Eryximachus and Phaedrus and
some of the others went off then, while he fell asleep for

a very long time, because the nights were long at that time of year. He woke up when it was nearly dawn and the cocks were already crowing. Once he'd woken up, he saw that the others were either asleep or had left, and that Agathon, Aristophanes and Socrates were the only ones still awake, drinking from a large bowl that they passed from left to right. Socrates was engaged in dialogue with them. Aristodemus said he couldn't remember most of the argument, because he'd missed the start and was half-asleep anyway. But the key point, he said, was that Socrates was pressing them to agree that the same man should be capable of writing both comedy and tragedy, and that anyone who is an expert in writing tragedy must also be an expert in writing comedy. He was getting them to agree this, though they were sleepy and not following very well; Aristophanes fell asleep first, and Agathon fell asleep when day was already breaking.

After getting them off to sleep, Socrates got up and went off. Aristodemus followed him as usual. Socrates went to the Lyceum, had a wash, spent the rest of the day as he did at other times, and only then in the evening went home to bed.

The Allegory of the Cave

1. Socrates begins with a reminder of the qualities of character which the philosopher must have, and goes on to emphasize that those qualities must be based on knowledge, ultimately on knowledge of the good, which for him means, as this passage makes clear, the form of the good. After dismissing briefly the views of those who believe the good is pleasure or knowledge, Socrates refuses to give a direct statement of his own view of it, and instead offers to describe it in a simile.

'Well, then, that part of our job is done – and it's not been easy; we must now go on to the next, and ask about the studies and pursuits which will produce these saviours of our society. What are they to learn and at what age are they to learn it?'

'Yes, that's our next question.'

'I didn't really gain anything,' I said, 'by being clever and putting off the difficulties about the possession of women, the production of children and the establishment of Rulers till later. I knew that my true society would give offence and be difficult to realize; but I have had to describe it all the same. I've dealt with the business about women and children, and now I've got to start again on the Rulers. You will remember that we said they must love their country, and be tested both in pleasure and pain, to ensure that their loyalty remained unshaken by pain or fear or any other vicissitude; those who failed the test were to be rejected, but those who emerged unscathed, like gold tried in the fire, were to be established as rulers and given honours and rewards both in life and after death. This is roughly what we said, but we were afraid of stirring up the problems we are now facing, and our argument evaded the issue and tried to get by without being seen.'

'Yes, I remember,' he said.

'You know, I hesitated before to say the rash things I've said,' I replied; 'but now let me be brave and say that our Guardians, in the fullest sense, must be philosophers.'

'So be it.'

'Think how few of them there are likely to be. The elements in the character which we said they must have don't usually combine into a whole, but are normally found separately.'

'What do you mean?'

'Readiness to learn and remember, quickness and keenness of mind and the qualities that go with them, and enterprise and breadth of vision, aren't usually combined with readiness to live an orderly, quiet and steady life; their keenness makes such temperaments very unpredictable and quite devoid of steadiness.'

'True.'

'And again, steady, consistent characters on whom you can rely, and who are unmoved by fear in war, are equally unmoved by instruction. Their immobility amounts indeed to numbness and, faced with anything that demands intellectual effort, they yawn and sink into slumber.'

'That's all quite true.'

'But we demand a full and fair share of both sets of qualities from anyone who is to be given the highest form of education and any share of office or authority.'

'And rightly.'

'So the character we want will be a rare occurrence.'

'It will.'

'And we must not only test it in the pains and fears and pleasures we have already described, but also try it out in a series of intellectual studies which we omitted before, to see if it has the endurance to pursue the highest forms of knowledge, without flinching as others flinch in physical trials.'

'A fair test; but what,' he asked, 'are these highest forms of knowledge?'

'You remember,' I answered, 'that we distinguished three elements in the mind, and then went on to deal with justice, self-control, courage and wisdom.'

'If I didn't remember that,' he said, 'I shouldn't have any claim to hear the rest of the argument.'

'Then do you remember what we said just before we dealt with these subjects?'

'What?'

'We said that a really clear view of them could only be got by making a detour for the purpose, though we could give some indication on the basis of our earlier argument. You said that was good enough, and so our subsequent description fell short, in my view, of real precision; whether it was precise enough for you, is for you to say.'

'I thought you gave us fair measure, and so, I think, did the others.'

'My dear Adeimantus, in matters like this nothing is fair measure that falls short of the truth in any respect,' I replied. 'You can't use the imperfect as a measure of anything – though people are sometimes content with it, and don't want to look further.'

'Yes, but it's usually because they're too lazy.'

'A most undesirable quality in a Guardian of state and laws.'

'A fair comment.'

'Then he must take the longer way round,' I said, 'and must work as hard at his intellectual training as at his physical; otherwise, as we've just said, he will never finally reach the highest form of knowledge, which should be peculiarly his own.'

'The highest?' he asked. 'But is there anything higher than justice and the other qualities we discussed?'

'There is,' I said. 'And we ought not to be content with the sight of a mere sketch even of these qualities, or fail to complete the picture in detail. For it would be absurd, would it not, to devote all our energies to securing the greatest possible precision and clarity in matters of little consequence, and not to demand the highest precision in the most important things of all?'

'Quite absurd,' he agreed. 'But you can hardly expect to escape cross-questioning about what you call the highest form of knowledge and its object.'

'I don't expect to escape from you,' I returned; 'ask

your questions. Though you've heard about it often enough, and either don't understand for the moment, or else are deliberately giving me trouble by your persistence – I suspect it's the latter, because you have certainly often been told that the highest form of knowledge is knowledge of the form of the good, from which things that are just and so on derive their usefulness and value. You know pretty well that that's what I have to say, and that I'm going to add that our knowledge of it is inadequate, and that if we are ignorant of it the rest of our knowledge, however perfect, can be of no benefit to us, just as it's no use possessing *anything* if you can't get any good out of it. Or do you think there's any point in possessing anything if it's no good? Is there any point in having all other forms of knowledge without that of the good, and so lacking knowledge about what is good and valuable?'

'I certainly don't think there is.'

'And you know of course that most ordinary people think that pleasure is the good, while the more sophisticated think it is knowledge.'

'Yes.'

'But those who hold this latter view can't tell us what knowledge they mean, but are compelled in the end to say they mean knowledge of the good.'

'Which is quite absurd.'

'An absurdity they can't avoid, if, after criticizing us for *not* knowing the good, they then turn round and talk to us as if we *did* know it; for they say it is "knowledge of the good" as if we understood what they meant when they utter the word "good".'

'That's perfectly true.'

'Then what about those who define good as pleasure? Is their confusion any less? Aren't they compelled to admit that there are bad pleasures?'

'Of course they are.'

'And they thus find themselves admitting that the same things are both good and bad, don't they?'

'Yes.'

'So it's obvious that the subject is highly controversial.'

'It is indeed.'

'Well, then, isn't it obvious too that when it's a matter of justice or value many people prefer the appearance to the reality, whether it's a matter of possession and action or of reputation; but that no one is satisfied to have something that only *appears* to be good, but wants something that *really* is, and has no use here for appearances?'

'Absolutely true.'

'The good, then, is the end of all endeavour, the object on which every heart is set, whose existence it divines, though it finds it difficult to grasp just what it is; and because it can't handle it with the same assurance as other things it misses any value those other things have. Can we possibly agree that the best of our citizens, to whom we are going to entrust everything, should be in the dark about so important a subject?'

'It's the last thing we can admit.'

'At any rate a man will not be a very useful Guardian of what is right and valuable if he does not know in what their goodness consists; and I suspect that until he does no one can know them adequately.'

'Your suspicions are well founded.'

'So our society will be properly regulated only if it is in the charge of a Guardian who has this knowledge.'

'That must be so,' he said. 'But what about you, Socrates? Do you think that the good is knowledge or pleasure? Or do you think it's something else?'

'What a man!' I exclaimed. 'It's been obvious for some time that you wouldn't be satisfied with other people's opinions!'

'But I don't think it's right, Socrates,' he protested, 'for you to be able to tell us other people's opinions but not your own, when you've given so much time to the subject.'

'Yes, but do you think it's right for a man to talk as if he knows what he does not?'

'He has no right to talk as if he knew; but he should be prepared to say what it is that he thinks.'

'Well,' I said, 'haven't you noticed that opinion without knowledge is always a poor thing? At the best it is blind – isn't anyone who holds a true opinion without understanding like a blind man on the right road?'

'Yes.'

'Then do you want a poor, blind, halting display from me, when you can get splendidly clear accounts from other people?'

'Now, for goodness' sake don't give up when you're just at the finish, Socrates,' begged Glaucon. 'We shall be quite satisfied if you give an account of the good similar to that you gave of justice and self-control and the rest.'

'And so shall I too, my dear chap,' I replied, 'but I'm afraid it's beyond me, and if I try I shall only make a fool of myself and be laughed at. So please let us give up asking for the present what the good is in itself; I'm afraid that to reach what I think would be a satisfactory answer is beyond the range of our present inquiry. But I will tell you, if you like, about something which seems to me to be a child of the good, and to resemble it very closely – or would you rather I didn't?'

'Tell us about the child and you can owe us your account of the parent,' he said.

'It's a debt I wish I could pay back to you in full, instead of only paying interest on the loan,' I replied. 'But for the present you must accept my description of the child of the good as interest. But take care I don't inadvertently cheat you by forging my account of the interest due.'

'We'll be as careful as we can,' he said. 'Go on.'

2. *The Simile of the Sun* [. . .]

'I must first get your agreement to, and remind you of, something we have said earlier in our discussion, and indeed on many other occasions.'

'What is it?' he asked.

I replied, 'We say that there are many particular things that are beautiful, and many that are good, and so on, and distinguish between them in our account.'

'Yes, we do.'

'And we go on to speak of beauty-in-itself, and goodness-in-itself, and so on for all the sets of particular things which we have regarded as many; and we proceed to posit by contrast a single form, which is unique, in each case, and call it "what really is" each thing.'

'That is so.'

'And we say that the particulars are objects of sight but not of intelligence, while the forms are the objects of intelligence but not of sight.'

'Certainly.'

'And with what part of ourselves do we see what we see?'

'With our sight.'

'And we hear with our hearing, and so on with the other senses and their objects.'

'Of course.'

'Then have you noticed,' I asked, 'how extremely lavish the designer of our senses was when he gave us the faculty of sight and made objects visible?'

'I can't say I have.'

'Then look. Do hearing and sound need something of another kind in addition to themselves to enable the ear to hear and the sound to be heard – some third element without which the one cannot hear or the other be heard?'

'No.'

'And the same is true of most, I might say all, the other senses. Or can you think of any that needs anything of the kind?'

'No, I can't.'

'But haven't you noticed that sight and the visible do need one?'

'How?'

'If the eyes have the power of sight, and its possessor tries to use this power, and if objects have colour, yet you know that he will see nothing and the colours will remain invisible unless a third element is present which is specifically and naturally adapted for the purpose.'

'What is that?' he asked.

'What you call light,' I answered.

'True.'

'Then the sense of sight and the visibility of objects are yoked by a yoke a long way more precious than any other – that is, if light is a precious thing.'

'Which it most certainly is.'

'Which, then, of the heavenly bodies do you regard as responsible for this? Whose light would you say it is that makes our eyes see and objects be seen most perfectly?'

'I should say the same as you or anyone else; you mean the sun, of course.'

'Then is sight related to its divine source as follows?'

'How?'

'The sun is not identical with sight, nor with what we call the eye in which sight resides.'

'No.'

'Yet of all sense-organs the eye is the most sunlike.'

'Much the most.'

'So the eye's power of sight is a kind of infusion dispensed to it by the sun.'

'Yes.'

'Then, moreover, though the sun is not itself sight, it is the cause of sight and is seen by the sight it causes.'

'That is so.'

'Well, that is what I called the child of the good,' I said. 'The good has begotten it in its own likeness, and it bears the same relation to sight and visible objects in the visible realm that the good bears to intelligence and intelligible objects in the intelligible realm.'

'Will you explain that a bit further?' he asked.

'You know that when we turn our eyes to objects whose colours are no longer illuminated by daylight, but only by moonlight or starlight, they see dimly and appear to be almost blind, as if they had no clear vision.'

'Yes.'

'But when we turn them on things on which the sun is shining, then they see clearly, and obviously have vision.'

'Certainly.'

'Apply the analogy to the mind. When the mind's eye is fixed on objects illuminated by truth and reality, it understands and knows them, and its possession of intelligence is evident; but when it is fixed on the twilight world of change and decay, it can only form opinions, its vision is confused and its opinions shifting, and it seems to lack intelligence.'

'That is true.'

'Then what gives the objects of knowledge their truth and the knower's mind the power of knowing is the form of the good. It is the cause of knowledge and truth, and you will be right to think of it as being itself known, and yet as being something other than, and even more splendid than, knowledge and truth, splendid as they are. And just as it was right to think of light and sight as being like the sun, but wrong to think of them as being the sun itself, so here again it is right to think of knowledge and truth as being like the good, but wrong to think of either of them as being the good, whose position must be ranked still higher.'

'You are making it something of remarkable splendour if it is the source of knowledge and truth, and yet itself more splendid than they are. For I suppose *you* can't mean it to be pleasure?' he asked.

'A monstrous suggestion,' I replied. 'Let us pursue our analogy further.'

'Go on.'

'The sun, I think you will agree, not only makes the things we see visible, but causes the processes of generation, growth and nourishment, without itself being such a process.'

'True.'

'The good therefore may be said to be the source not only of the intelligibility of the objects of knowledge, but also of their being and reality; yet it is not itself that reality, but is beyond it, and superior to it in dignity and power.'

'It really must be miraculously transcendent,' remarked Glaucon to the general amusement.

'Now, don't blame me,' I protested; 'it was you who made me say what I thought about it.'

'Yes, and please go on. At any rate finish off the analogy with the sun, if you haven't finished it.'

'I've not nearly finished it.'

'Then go on and don't leave anything out.'

'I'm afraid I must leave a lot out,' I said. 'But I'll do my best to get in everything I can in present circumstances.'

'Yes, please do.'

The Divided Line

The analogy of the Divided Line is, Plato makes clear, a sequel to the Sun simile, its purpose being to illustrate further the relation between the two orders of reality with which the Sun simile dealt. But it does so from a particular point of view, that of the states of mind in which we apprehend these two orders or realms. The purpose of the Line, therefore, is not, primarily, to give a classification of objects. Both of the two states of mind correlated with the intelligible realm deal with the same kind of object (the forms), though each deals with them in a different way; and though in the physical world there is a difference between physical things and their shadows, that difference is used primarily to illustrate degrees of 'truth' or genuineness in what is apprehended – we know very little about a thing if our knowledge is confined to shadows or images of it or, for that matter, to its superficial appearance [. . .]

'You must suppose, then,' I went on, 'that there are these two powers of which I have spoken, and that one of them is supreme over everything in the intelligible order or region, the other over everything in the visible region – I won't say in the physical universe or you will think I'm playing with words. At any rate you have before your mind these two orders of things, the visible and the intelligible?'

'Yes, I have.'

'Well, suppose you have a line divided into two unequal parts, and then divide the two parts again in the same ratio, to represent the visible and intelligible orders. This gives you, in terms of comparative clarity and obscurity, in the visible order one sub-section of images: by "images" I mean first shadows, then reflections in water and other close-grained, polished surfaces, and all that sort of thing, if you understand me.'

'I understand.'

'Let the other sub-section stand for the objects which are the originals of the images – the animals around us, and every kind of plant and manufactured object.'

'Very good.'

'Would you be prepared to admit that these sections differ in that one is genuine, one not, and that the relation of image to original is the same as that of the realm of opinion to that of knowledge?'

'I most certainly would.'

'Then consider next how the intelligible part of the line is to be divided.'

'How?'

'In one sub-section the mind uses the originals of the visible order in their turn as images, and has to base its inquiries on assumptions and proceed from them not to a first principle but to a conclusion: in the other it moves from assumption to a first principle which involves no assumption, without the images used in the other sub-section, but pursuing its inquiry solely by and through forms themselves.'

'I don't quite understand.'

'I will try again, and what I have just said will help you to understand. I think you know that students of geometry and calculation and the like begin by assuming there are odd and even numbers, geometrical figures and the three forms of angle, and other kindred items in their respective subjects; these they regard as known, having put them forward as basic assumptions which it is quite unnecessary to explain to themselves or anyone else on the grounds that they are obvious to everyone. Starting from them, they proceed through a series of consistent steps to the conclusion which they set out to find.'

'Yes, I certainly know that.'

'You know too that they make use of and argue about visible figures, though they are not really thinking about them, but about the originals which they resemble; it is *not* about the square or diagonal which they have drawn that they are arguing, but about the square itself or diagonal itself, or whatever the figure may be. The actual figures they draw or model, which themselves cast their shadows and reflections in water – these they treat as images only, the real objects of their investigation being invisible except to the eye of reason.'

'That is quite true.'

'This type of thing I called intelligible, but said that the mind was forced to use assumptions in investigating it, and did not proceed to a first principle, being unable to depart from and rise above its assumptions; but it used as illustrations the very things which in turn have their images and shadows on the lower level, in comparison with which they are themselves respected and valued for their clarity.'

'I understand,' he said. 'You are referring to what happens in geometry and kindred sciences.'

'Then when I speak of the other sub-section of the intelligible part of the line you will understand that I mean that which the very process of argument grasps by the power of dialectic; it treats assumptions not as principles, but as assumptions in the true sense, that is, as starting points and steps in the ascent to something which involves no assumption and is the first principle of everything; when it has grasped that principle it can again descend, by keeping to the consequences that follow from it, to a conclusion. The whole procedure involves nothing in the sensible world, but moves solely through forms to forms, and finishes with forms.'

'I understand,' he said; 'though not fully, because what you describe sounds like a long job. But you want to distinguish that part of the real and intelligible which is studied by the science of dialectic as having greater clarity than that studied by what are called "sciences". These sciences treat their assumptions as first principles and, though compelled to use reason and not sense-perception in surveying their subject-matter, because they proceed in their investigations *from* assumptions and not *to* a first principle, they do not, you think, exercise intelligence on it, even though with the aid of a first principle it is intelligible. And I think that you call the habit of mind of geometers and the like reason but not intelligence, meaning by reason something midway between opinion and intelligence.'

'You have understood me very well,' I said. 'So please take it that there are, corresponding to the four sections of the line, these four states of mind; to the top section intelligence, to the second reason, to the third belief, and to the last illusion. And you may arrange them in a scale, and assume that they have degrees of clarity corresponding to the degree of truth possessed by their subject-matter.'

'I understand,' he replied, 'and agree with your proposed arrangement.'

The Simile of the Cave

This is a more graphic presentation of the truths presented in the analogy of the Line; in particular, it tells us more about the two states of mind called in the Line analogy Belief and Illusion. We are shown the ascent of the mind from illusion to pure philosophy, and the difficulties which accompany its progress. And the philosopher, when he has achieved the supreme vision, is required to return to the cave and serve his fellows, his very unwillingness to do so being his chief qualification [. . .]

'I want you to go on to picture the enlightenment or ignorance of our human condition somewhat as follows. Imagine an underground chamber like a cave, with a long entrance open to the daylight and as wide as the cave. In this chamber are men who have been prisoners there since they were children, their legs and necks being so fastened that they can only look straight ahead of them and cannot turn their heads. Some way off, behind and higher up, a fire is burning, and between the fire and the prisoners and above them runs a road, in front of which a curtain-wall has been built, like the screen at puppet shows between the operators and their audience, above which they show their puppets.'

'I see.'

'Imagine further that there are men carrying all sorts of gear along behind the curtain-wall, projecting above it and including figures of men and animals made of wood and stone and all sorts of other materials, and that some of these men, as you would expect, are talking and some not.'

'An odd picture and an odd sort of prisoner.'

'They are drawn from life,' I replied. 'For, tell me, do you think our prisoners could see anything of themselves or their fellows except the shadows thrown by the fire on the wall of the cave opposite them?'

'How could they see anything else if they were prevented from moving their heads all their lives?'

'And would they see anything more of the objects carried along the road?'

'Of course not.'

'Then if they were able to talk to each other, would they not assume that the shadows they saw were the real things?'

'Inevitably.'

'And if the wall of their prison opposite them reflected sound, don't you think that they would suppose, whenever one of the passers-by on the road spoke, that the voice belonged to the shadow passing before them?'

'They would be bound to think so.'

'And so in every way they would believe that the shadows of the objects we mentioned were the whole truth.'

'Yes, inevitably.'

'Then think what would naturally happen to them if they were released from their bonds and cured of their delusions. Suppose one of them were let loose, and suddenly compelled to stand up and turn his head and look and walk towards the fire; all these actions would be painful and he would be too dazzled to see properly the objects of which he used to see the shadows. What do you think he would say if he was told that what he used to see was so much empty nonsense and that he was now nearer reality and seeing more correctly, because he was turned towards objects that were more real, and if on top of that he were compelled to say what each of the passing objects was when it was pointed out to him? Don't you think he would be at a loss, and think that what he used to see was far truer than the objects now being pointed out to him?'

'Yes, far truer.'

'And if he were made to look directly at the light of the fire, it would hurt his eyes and he would turn back and retreat to the things which he could see properly, which he would think really clearer than the things being shown him.'

'Yes.'

'And if,' I went on, 'he were forcibly dragged up the steep and rugged ascent and not let go till he had been dragged out into the sunlight, the process would be a painful one, to which he would much object, and when he emerged into the light his eyes would be so dazzled by the glare of it that he wouldn't be able to see a single one of the things he was now told were real.'

'Certainly not at first,' he agreed.

'Because, of course, he would need to grow accustomed to the light before he could see things in the upper world outside the cave. First he would find it easiest to look at shadows, next at the reflections of men and other objects in water, and later on at the objects themselves. After that he would find it easier to observe the heavenly bodies and the sky itself at night, and to look at the light of the moon and stars rather than at the sun and its light by day.'

'Of course.'

'The thing he would be able to do last would be to look directly at the sun itself, and gaze at it without using reflections in water or any other medium, but as it is in itself.'

'That must come last.'

'Later on he would come to the conclusion that it is the sun that produces the changing seasons and years and controls everything in the visible world, and is in a sense responsible for everything that he and his fellow-prisoners used to see.'

'That is the conclusion which he would obviously reach.'

'And when he thought of his first home and what passed for wisdom there, and of his fellow-prisoners, don't you think he would congratulate himself on his good fortune and be sorry for them?'

'Very much so.'

'There was probably a certain amount of honour and glory to be won among the prisoners, and prizes for keensightedness for those best able to remember the order of sequence among the passing shadows and so be best able to divine their future appearances. Will our released prisoner hanker after these prizes or envy this power or honour? Won't he be more likely to feel, as Homer says, that he would far rather be "a serf in the house of some landless man", or indeed anything else in the world, than hold the opinions and live the life that they do?'

'Yes,' he replied, 'he would prefer anything to a life like theirs.'

'Then what do you think would happen,' I asked, 'if he went back to sit in his old seat in the cave? Wouldn't his eyes be blinded by the darkness, because he had come in suddenly out of the sunlight?'

'Certainly.'

'And if he had to discriminate between the shadows, in competition with the other prisoners, while he was still blinded and before his eyes got used to the darkness – a process that would take some time – wouldn't he be likely to make a fool of himself? And they would say that his visit to the upper world had ruined his sight, and that the ascent was not worth even attempting. And if anyone tried to release them and lead them up, they would kill him if they could lay hands on him.'

'They certainly would.'

'Now, my dear Glaucon,' I went on, 'this simile must be connected throughout with what preceded it. The realm revealed by sight corresponds to the prison, and the light of the fire in the prison to the power of the sun. And you won't go wrong if you connect the ascent into the upper world and the sight of the objects there with the upward progress of the mind into the intelligible region. That at any rate is my interpretation, which is what you are anxious to hear; the truth of the matter is, after all, known only to god. But in my opinion, for what it is worth, the final thing to be perceived in the intelligible region, and perceived only with difficulty, is the form of the good; once seen, it is inferred to be responsible for whatever is right and valuable in anything, producing in the visible region light and the source of light, and being in the intelligible region itself the controlling source of truth and intelligence. And anyone who is going to act rationally either in public or private life must have sight of it.'

'I agree,' he said, 'so far as I am able to understand you.'

'Then you will perhaps also agree with me that it won't be surprising if those who get so far are unwilling to involve themselves in human affairs, and if their minds long to remain in the realm above. That's what we should expect if our simile holds good again.'

'Yes, that's to be expected.'

'Nor will you think it strange that anyone who descends from contemplation of the divine to human life and its ills should blunder and make a fool of himself, if, while still blinded and unaccustomed to the surrounding darkness, he's forcibly put on trial in the law-courts or elsewhere about the shadows of justice or the figures of which they are shadows, and made to dispute about the notions of them held by men who have never seen justice itself.'

'There's nothing strange in that.'

'But anyone with any sense,' I said, 'will remember that the eyes may be unsighted in two ways, by a transition either from light to darkness or from darkness to light, and will recognize that the same thing applies to the mind. So when he sees a mind confused and unable to see clearly he will not laugh without thinking, but will ask himself whether it has come from a clearer world and is confused by the unaccustomed darkness, or whether it is dazzled by the stronger light of the clearer world to which it has escaped from its previous ignorance. The first condition of life is a reason for congratulation, the second for sympathy, though if one wants to laugh at it one can do so with less absurdity than at the mind that has descended from the daylight of the upper world.'

'You put it very reasonably.'

'If this is true,' I continued, 'we must reject the conception of education professed by those who say that they can put into the mind knowledge that was not there before – rather as if they could put sight into blind eyes.'

'It is a claim that is certainly made,' he said.

'But our argument indicates that the capacity for knowledge is innate in each man's mind, and that the organ by which he learns is like an eye which cannot be turned from darkness to light unless the whole body is turned; in the same way the mind as a whole must be turned away from the world of change until its eye can bear to look straight at reality, and at the brightest of all realities which is what we call the good. Isn't that so?'

'Yes.'

'Then this turning around of the mind itself might be made a subject of professional skill, which would effect the conversion as easily and effectively as possible. It would not be concerned to implant sight, but to ensure that someone who had it already was not either turned in the wrong direction or looking the wrong way.'

'That may well be so.'

'The rest, therefore, of what are commonly called excellences of the mind perhaps resemble those of the body, in that they are not in fact innate, but are implanted by subsequent training and practice; but knowledge, it seems, must surely have a diviner quality, something which never loses its power, but whose effects are useful and salutary or again useless and harmful according to the direction in which it is turned. Have you never noticed how shrewd is the glance of the type of men commonly called bad but clever? They have small minds, but their sight is sharp and piercing enough in matters that concern them; it's not that their sight is weak, but that they are forced to serve evil, so that the keener their sight the more effective that evil is.'

'That's true.'

'But suppose,' I said, 'that such natures were cut loose, when they were still children, from all the dead weights natural to this world of change and fastened on them by sensual indulgences like gluttony, which twist their minds' vision to lower things, and suppose that when so freed they were turned towards the truth, then this same part of these same individuals would have as keen a vision of truth as it has of the objects on which it is at present turned.'

'Very likely.'

'And is it not also likely, and indeed a necessary consequence of what we have said, that society will never be properly governed either by the uneducated, who have no knowledge of the truth, or by those who are allowed to spend all their lives in purely intellectual pursuits? The uneducated have no single aim in life to which all their actions, public and private, are to be directed; the intellectuals will take no practical action of their own accord, fancying themselves to be out of this world in some kind of earthly paradise.'

'True.'

'Then our job as lawgivers is to compel the best minds to attain what we have called the highest form of knowledge, and to ascend to the vision of the good as we have described, and when they have achieved this and see well enough, prevent them behaving as they are now allowed to.'

'What do you mean by that?'

'Remaining in the upper world, and refusing to return again to the prisoners in the cave below and share their labours and rewards, whether trivial or serious.'

'But surely,' he protested, 'that will not be fair. We shall be compelling them to live a poorer life than they might live.'

'The object of our legislation,' I reminded him again, 'is not the special welfare of any particular class in our society, but of the society as a whole; and it uses persuasion or compulsion to unite all citizens and make them share together the benefits which each individually can confer on the community; and its purpose in fostering this attitude is not to leave everyone to please himself, but to make each man a link in the unity of the whole.'

'You are right; I had forgotten,' he said.

'You see, then, Glaucon,' I went on, 'we shan't be unfair to our philosophers, but shall be quite fair in what we say when we compel them to have some care and responsibility for others. We shall tell them that philosophers born in other states can reasonably refuse to take part in the hard work of politics; for society produces them quite involuntarily and unintentionally, and it is only just that anything that grows up on its own should feel it has nothing to repay for an upbringing which it owes to no one. "But," we shall say, "we have bred you both for your own sake and that of the whole community to act as leaders and king-bees in a hive; you are better and more fully educated than the rest and better qualified to combine the practice of philosophy and politics. You must therefore each descend in turn and live with your fellows in the cave and get used to seeing in the dark; once you get used to it you will see a thousand times better than they do and will distinguish the various shadows, and know what they are shadows of, because you have seen the truth about things admirable and just and good. And so our state and yours will be really awake, and not merely dreaming like most societies today, with their shadow battles and their struggles for political power, which they treat as some great prize. The truth is quite different: the state whose prospective rulers come to their duties with least enthusiasm is bound to have the best and most tranquil government, and the state whose rulers are eager to rule the worst." '

'I quite agree.'

'Then will our pupils, when they hear what we say, dissent and refuse to take their share of the hard work of government, even though spending the greater part of their time together in the pure air above?'

'They cannot refuse, for we are making a just demand of just men. But of course, unlike present rulers, they will approach the business of government as an unavoidable necessity.'

'Yes, of course,' I agreed. 'The truth is that if you want a well-governed state to be possible, you must find for your future rulers some way of life they like better than government; for only then will you have government by the truly rich, those, that is, whose riches consist not of gold, but of the true happiness of a good and rational life. If you get, in public affairs, men whose life is impoverished and destitute of personal satisfactions, but who hope to snatch some compensation for their own inadequacy from a political career, there can never be good government. They start fighting for power, and the consequent internal and domestic conflicts ruin both them and society.'

'True indeed.'

'Is there any life except that of true philosophy which looks down on positions of political power?'

'None whatever.'

'But what we need is that the only men to get power should be men who do not love it, otherwise we shall have rivals' quarrels.'

'That is certain.'

'Who else, then, will you compel to undertake the

responsibilities of Guardians of our state, if it is not to be those who know most about the principles of good government and who have other rewards and a better life than the politician's?'

'There is no one else.'